# HOW TO DO just about ANYTHING IN Microsoft® PowerPoint

READER'S DIGEST

# HOW TO DO just about ANYTHING IN Microsoft® PowerPoint

Published by The Reader's Digest Association Limited
London • New York • Sydney • Montreal

**For Reader's Digest**

**Editor**
Caroline Boucher

**Art Editor**
Conorde Clarke

**Assistant editor**
Rachel Weaver

**Designer**
Wai Sing Tang

**Technical Consultant**
Tony Rilett

**Proofreader**
Barry Gage

**Index**
Nigel d'Auvergne

**Reader's Digest General Books**

**Editorial Director**
Julian Browne

**Art Director**
Anne-Marie Bulat

**Head of Book Development**
Sarah Bloxham

**Managing Editor**
Nina Hathway

**Picture Resource Manager**
Sarah Stewart-Richardson

**Pre-press Account Manager**
Dean Russell

**Production Controller**
Sandra Fuller

**Product Production Manager**
Claudette Bramble

*How to do just about anything in Microsoft® PowerPoint* was adapted from *Microsoft PowerPoint Gewusst Wie!*, published by Reader's Digest (Germany).

**Acknowledgments**

We would like to thank the following individuals and organisations for their assistance in producing this book.

Photography: Karl Adamson
Equipment: Dell Computer Corporation

# Contents

## Basics

## Creating your Presentation

## Automating Tasks

## Embedding Objects

## Organising your Presentation

## Presentation Perfect

## Advanced Techniques

# How to use this book

This book will show you how to create clear, informative and engaging presentations using Microsoft PowerPoint 2007. Each project is set out with simple step-by-step instructions, helpful tips and pictures showing you exactly what you'll see on screen. With this helpful guide, you'll soon be creating professional-looking presentations which are perfect for any audience.

## GETTING AROUND THE BOOK

**This book covers all the key features of PowerPoint, starting with the basics and moving on to more advanced tasks. You can work through each section in order, or dip in and out of the book.**

### Basics

This is essential reading for those new to PowerPoint. Get to grips with the fundamentals of using PowerPoint and create, save and print your first presentation.

### Creating your presentation

Here you'll find everything you need to know to produce a successful PowerPoint presentation.

### Automating tasks

Are you fed up with repeating the same tasks again and again? This chapter shows you how to get PowerPoint to do them for you.

### Embedding media files

Give your presentation a professional touch by inserting a chart, an eye-catching diagram, or even some background music or sound effects.

### Organising your presentation

Find out how to structure your presentations and how to include personal notes within your PowerPoint document.

### Presentation perfect

For your presentation to be a real success, you need to present it in the most effective way possible to your audience. You'll find all the help you need in this chapter.

### Advanced techniques

If you are up to speed with the basics, the advanced techniques in this section will show you how to master some of the more complex techniques in PowerPoint.

## WHICH SOFTWARE VERSION

The information in this book is based on a PC using Microsoft PowerPoint 2007 (part of the Office 2007 Small Business edition) and Windows Vista Home Premium.

If you already have an earlier version of Office installed on your computer, you can upgrade it to this newer version and this will give you access to Microsoft PowerPoint 2007. If PowerPoint is a completely new program for your computer, you will need to install the Office suite from scratch.

**Close-up**
***These project-specific tips offer you extra detail on various PowerPoint functions.***

**Bright idea**
***Wondering how to use your new-found skills? Look out for these tips.***

**Key word**
***You'll find handy definitions of technical words and phrases here.***

## GETTING AROUND THE PAGE

**You're guided through every task by means of illustrated steps and a range of visual features. Here are the key elements to look for on each page.**

### See also
Want to find out more? This panel points you towards other relevant projects for you to try.

### Step-by-step
Projects are set out in clear steps. You are instructed on the keyboard and mouse commands to give, and which buttons to click on.

### Useful tips
Explanations of the more complex aspects of a task and alternative ways to do things.

### Before you start
Projects begin with a short section of text. This outlines points to consider and any necessary preparatory work.

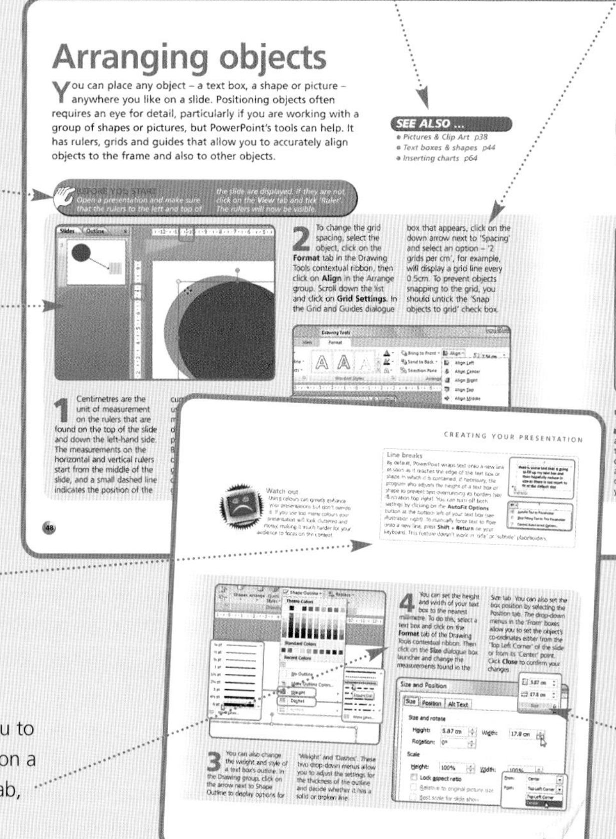


### Snapshots
Pictures of the PC screen – 'snapshots' – show you what you'll see on your own screen at each stage of the project.

### Comments
These boxes focus on a specific aspect of the task and explain it in greater detail.

### Bold type
Any bold text is a command for you to carry out. You might need to click on a toolbar button or a dialogue box tab, or press a key.

### Magnifications
Snapshots of the PC screen that require special attention are magnified so that you can see them more clearly.

### Page turns
The arrow indicates that your project continues over the page. Projects range from two pages to four.

### That's amazing!
Inspiring ideas and explanations, such as time-saving shortcuts, which you will find both interesting and useful.

### Watch out
These tips warn you of possible difficulties and pitfalls and give helpful advice on how to avoid problems.

### Expert advice
Advanced tips offer guidance on specific features and useful advice on how to get professional results.

# Set up your PC safely

When you are choosing a location for your PC, check that there is adequate space and several mains sockets for all of the equipment. You need to consider lighting and seating, and the amount of desk space available. If you want to connect to the Internet, you will also need to be near a telephone wall socket unless you have a wireless connection.

## SITTING AT YOUR COMPUTER

**You need to think carefully about how to arrange your area, as a poorly laid out computer desk and PC will be tiring to use and may prevent you from operating your computer properly.**

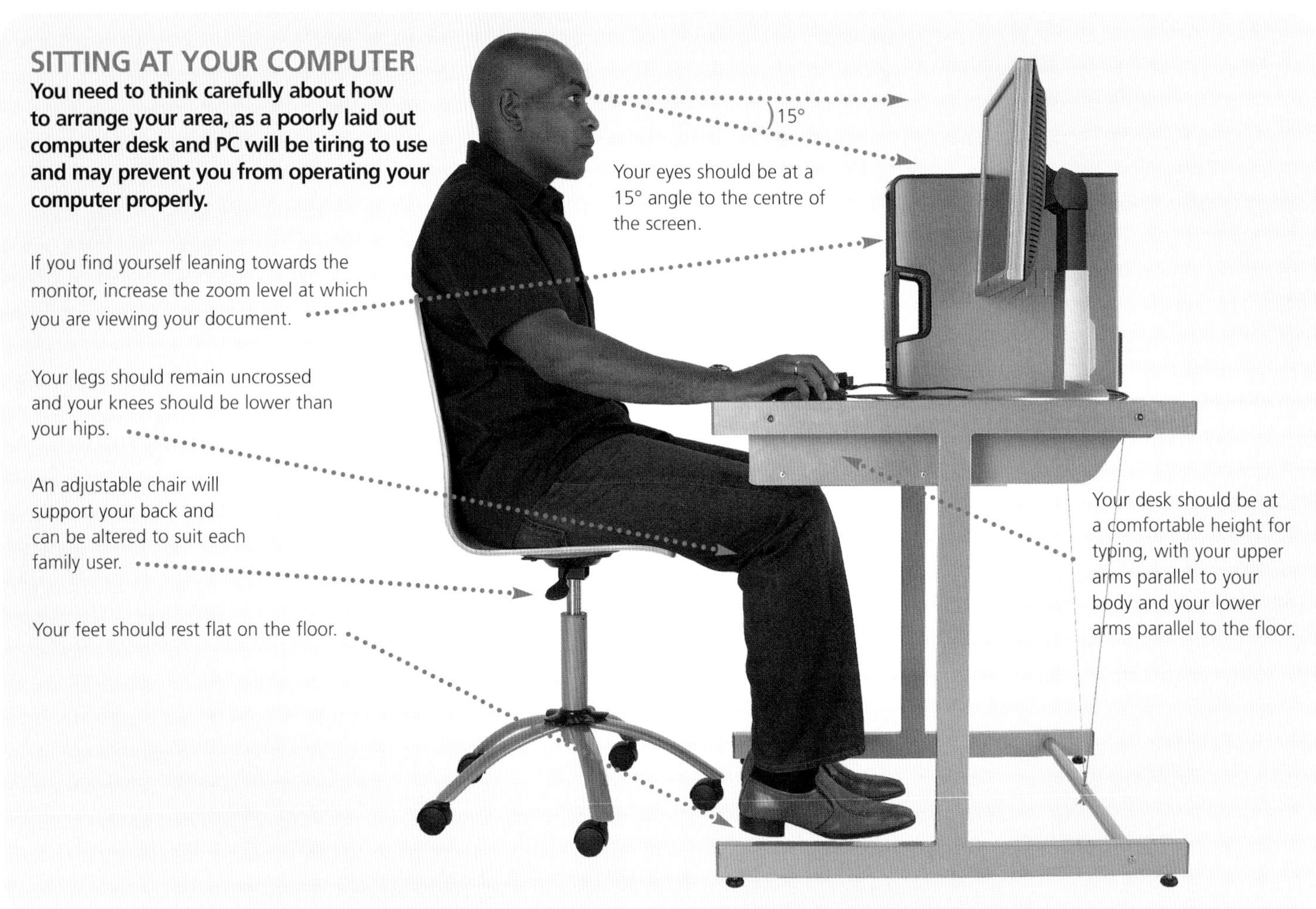

## NAMING AND PLACING PARTS

**Your PC's hardware includes all the parts that you can actually see and handle. Knowing how to position these elements ensures a safe and efficient work area.**

### System unit

This is the part of your computer to which everything is connected. Leave space so that you can plug in the cables easily and to allow for ventilation. Don't leave cables trailing.

### Monitor

This is the computer's screen. Position your monitor to avoid reflections, but do not face a bright window yourself as this may lead to eyestrain.

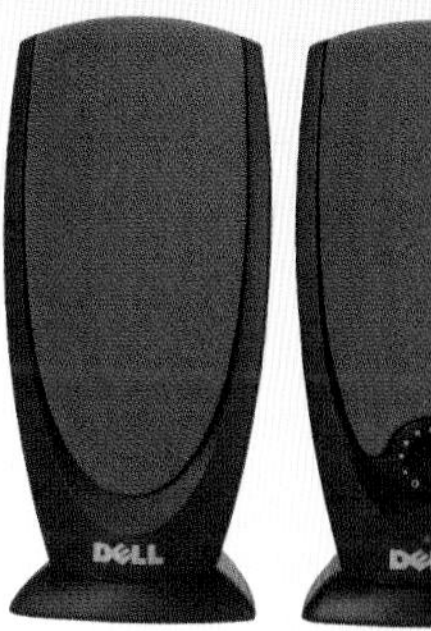


### Speakers

For the best sound quality, speakers should be placed on either side of the monitor and at desk level or higher, not just pushed under the desk.

### Printer

Position your printer near the system unit. Make sure there is sufficient space around it for loading the paper trays.

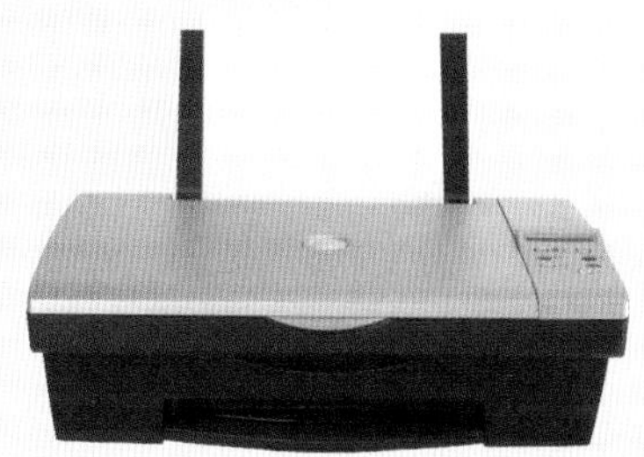

### Keyboard

Make sure the keyboard is on a stable and level surface within easy reach. Leave enough space in front of it for hands and wrists. Ensure that the desk is at the correct height.

### Mouse

Place the mouse to the side of your keyboard that suits whether you are left or right-handed. Use a mouse mat to create the correct amount of friction, and be sure there is plenty of room to move the mouse around.

### Expert advice

If you are planning to use your computer a lot, you should invest in a good-quality, comfortable office chair. Most dining chairs do not offer the support for your back that is important when you are sitting still for long periods. Also, most office chairs are adjustable, so can suit every member of the family. Remember, even with a comfortable chair, you should take regular 10 minute breaks to walk around.

# What is PowerPoint?

A presentation program enables you to create presentations using text and graphics. But with PowerPoint you can do so much more, producing interactive multimedia presentations using a mixture of diagrams, charts, special effects and even sound effects. PowerPoint puts this creative potential at your fingertips and makes it easy.


**SEE ALSO ...**

- *Formatting text* p32
- *Using themes* p52
- *Slide shows* p92


## HOW IT WORKS

**Slides are the essential components of a PowerPoint presentation. Use them to put the contents of your presentation in the order you wish to present them.**

Most presentations are essentially text-based. You can format the words in the same way that you format text in a word-processing program, using different type sizes, fonts, colours and even animated effects. PowerPoint's preset shapes, including stars and arrows, are particularly eye catching, and you can enter text in them.

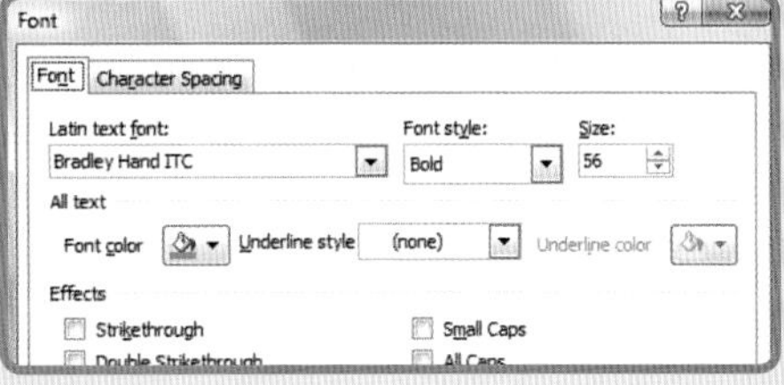


### Bring on the colour

Putting a coloured background behind your slides and using design elements are two ways to make sure your presentation is visually appealing to your audience. You don't need to be a graphic designer – it is easy to apply one of PowerPoint's ready-made themes, complete with colours and fonts. Another way to highlight certain points and make information more digestible is to use the many diagrams and chart styles that are available.

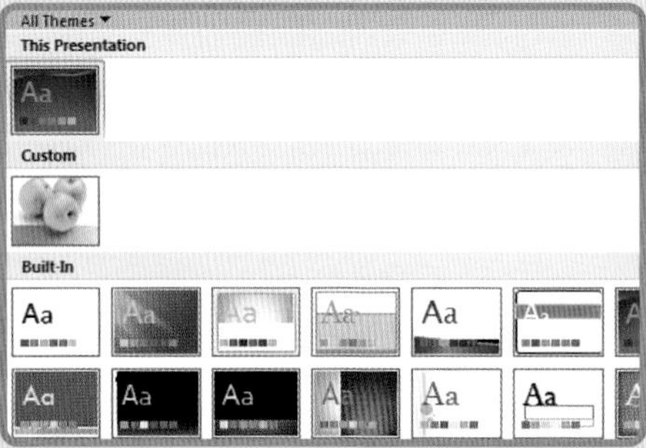


### Curtain up!

You can easily print out your finished presentation or, for more impact, you can project your slides on to a screen. If you do choose to use a projector, PowerPoint has a wide range of animations and special effects that can help to turn your basic slides into a multimedia event.

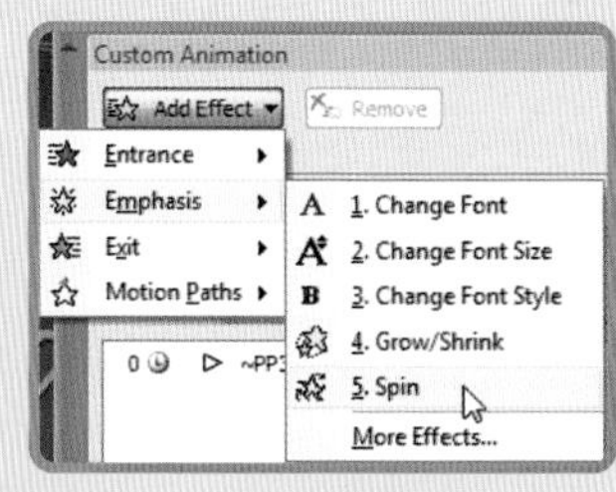


### A little extra help

Sometimes, you'll need some extra help – especially if you are new to PowerPoint. To access the help window, press F1.

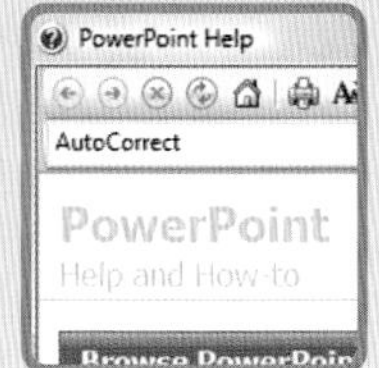


### PowerPoint and Microsoft Office

Although you can buy PowerPoint 2007 as a standalone application, most people buy it as part of the Microsoft Office suite, which also includes other programs. Exactly which other programs are included depends on which version of Office you buy. In addition to PowerPoint, the standard Small Business edition of Office includes the word-processing application Word, the spreadsheet program Excel and Outlook – an email program, calendar and address book. Other editions contain Access, which is a database management program.

## FIRST STEPS

**If you are not an experienced computer user, you'll need a few tips to help you to get started.**

### The mouse

You'll use the mouse for most of the things that you do in PowerPoint. Use it to move the mouse pointer around the screen, select and move objects and access all of PowerPoint's features through the program's Ribbon, dialogue boxes and toolbars. A Windows mouse has at least two buttons. Press the left button to 'click' and the right button to 'right-click'. To 'double-click', press the left button twice in close succession.

When you move the mouse pointer over text, it changes from a white selection arrow into an insertion point which looks like a capital 'I'. To

- Three magazines started in
- and Reader's Digest and this
- BBC. All are still with us
- The story began in a Greenw

press a button, move the mouse pointer over it and click on it.

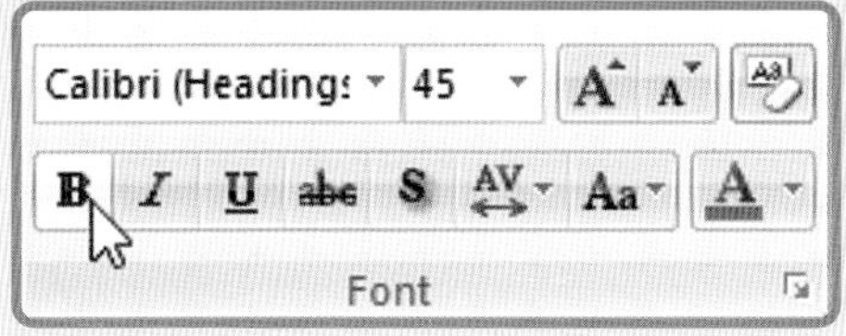


### Selecting objects

You can use the mouse to select any object in a presentation. For example, to select a section of text, place the cursor just before the first letter of the text, click the left mouse button and hold it down as you move the cursor in the direction you want. As you do so, the text you select is highlighted on a grey background. When all the text you want to select is highlighted, release the mouse button. If you only want to select a single word, simply double-click on it.

It's a similar process to select a picture or text box: move the mouse to the edge of the box and click the mouse button when a four-headed arrow appears. To move the object, hold the mouse button down as you 'drag' the object to its new position. Then, release the mouse button to 'drop' the object at that location.

### Browsing through the document

You can scroll through your document using the arrows on the scrollbars to the right or bottom of your screen. To move more quickly, click on the blue bar and drag it while holding down the left mouse button.

### The Ribbon

Near the top of the screen, below the Title bar, is the Ribbon. Through the tabs on the Ribbon you have access to a wide range of useful commands. Hover your mouse pointer over a button to display a 'pop-up' window showing the command that button performs. When you click

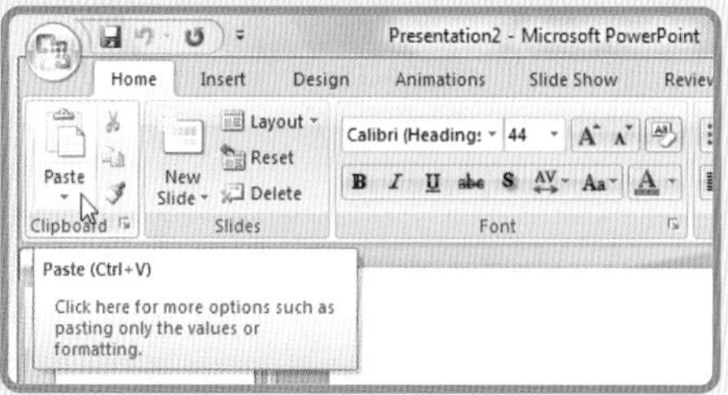


on buttons, such as 'Paste', found under the Home tab, a drop-down menu of options is displayed. If applicable, the keyboard shortcut that performs the action is also displayed (see list overleaf).

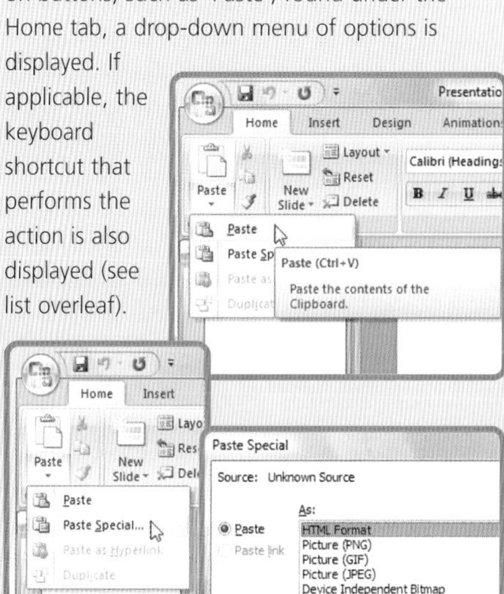


### Watch out!

Using PowerPoint 2007, you shouldn't have any difficulty opening presentations that were created in an earlier version of the software (for example PowerPoint 2003). However, the same is not true the other way around and you won't generally be able to open documents saved in PowerPoint 2007 format if you are using an older version of the program.

## USING THE KEYBOARD

**Function keys** are shortcuts to commands:
**F1** opens the Microsoft Help and Support screen.
**F4** repeats your last command.
**F5** starts a slide show, with the first slide filling the entire screen.
**F6** moves to the next slide.
**F7** checks a presentation for spelling and grammar.
**F12** allows you to create a copy of the presentation by saving it as a new file with a different file name.
**Esc** ends a slideshow.

**Delete** removes text that is selected or positioned to the right of the cursor.
**Home** displays the first slide of a presentation.
**End** displays the last slide of a presentation.
**Page Up** displays the previous slide.
**Page Down** displays the next slide.

**Caps Lock** makes all the letters that you type appear as capitals.
**Shift** allows you to type a letter as a capital or to select the top-marked option on a key. For example, pressing 'Shift' + '5' types the '%' symbol.
**Ctrl** and **Alt** keys, when pressed in conjunction with other keys, provides access to certain commands (keyboard shortcuts). For example, pressing 'Ctrl' + 'P' opens the Print dialogue box.
**Ctrl + Alt + Delete** is a useful way to quit PowerPoint if it stops responding.
**Windows key** accesses the Start menu.

**Spacebar** adds spaces between words.

**Return** creates a paragraph break or ends a line early.

**Backspace** deletes text to the left of your cursor.

**Arrow keys** move the cursor up, down, left and right.

**Enter keys** works like the Return key.

### USEFUL KEYBOARD SHORTCUTS

Keyboard shortcuts make working in PowerPoint easier. Here's a small selection:
**Ctrl + Z** undoes your last action.
**Ctrl + S** saves the active document.
**Ctrl + O** accesses the Open dialogue box.
**Ctrl + N** opens a new document.
**Ctrl + M** inserts a new slide.
**Ctrl + F** opens the Find dialogue box.
**Ctrl + D** duplicates a text or picture object.

Keyboard shortcuts are also very useful during a slide show:
**Spacebar** displays the next slide or animation in the presentation.
**Backspace** displays the previous slide or animation in the presentation.
**N** displays the next slide of the presentation.
**P** displays the previous slide or animation of the presentation.
**Number/s + Return** jumps to the slide number entered.
**W** displays a white screen.
**Ctrl + A** display the pointer arrows.
**Ctrl + H** hide the pointer arrows.

### Bright idea

***You can learn more about PowerPoint's keyboard shortcuts through the Help function. Enter 'keyboard shortcuts' in the text field in the top right of the screen and press the*** *Return* ***key.***

# Basics

# Explore the program

If you have ever used a word-processing program such as Word, finding your way around the PowerPoint workspace will be easy. But before you start creating a presentation, it is a good idea to take a moment to familiarise yourself with some of the program's tools and functions. This will provide you with a better understanding of the powerful features on offer.

**SEE ALSO ...**

- *What is PowerPoint?* p12
- *First steps* p20

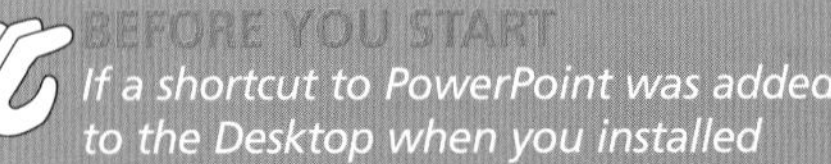

**BEFORE YOU START**

*If a shortcut to PowerPoint was added to the Desktop when you installed PowerPoint, start the program by simply double-clicking on the PowerPoint icon with the small arrow.*

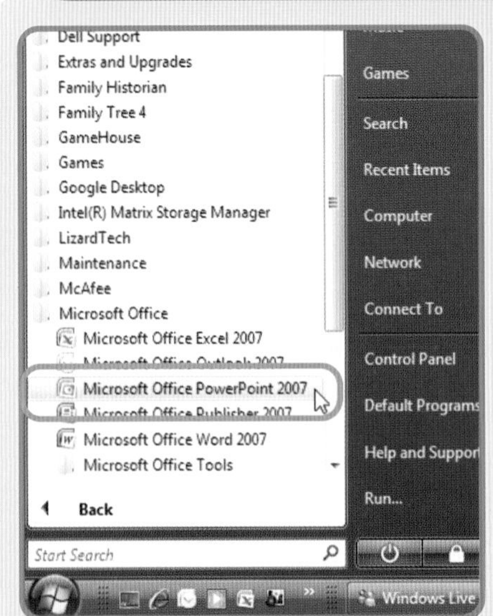


**1** If you don't have a shortcut to PowerPoint on your Desktop, click on the **Start** button and then on **Microsoft Office PowerPoint 2007**. If you can't see PowerPoint in the main menu, click on **All Programs**, then **Microsoft Office** and select it from the menu.

**2** A welcome screen will appear as the program starts up, telling you which version of PowerPoint you are using and displaying the copyright statement. If you have one of the newer computer models the information will only appear briefly before the main program window opens.

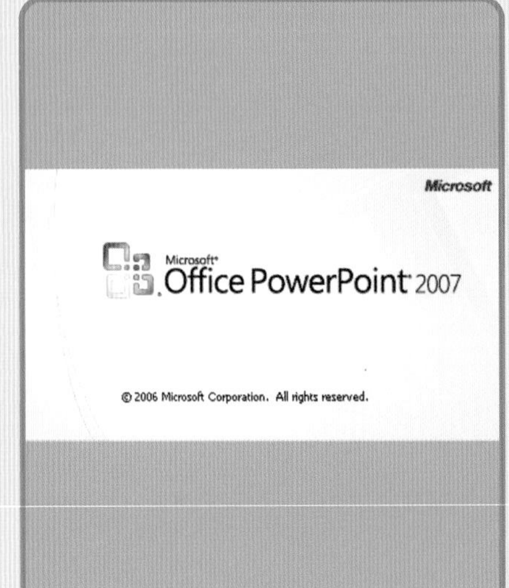


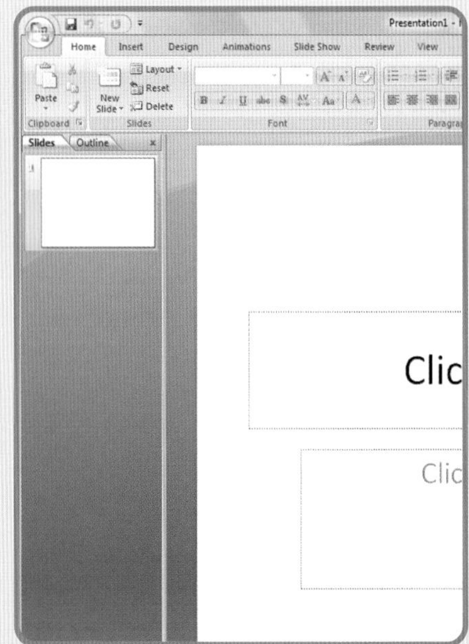


**3** Once PowerPoint has opened, a new blank presentation will appear on screen, into which you can start entering your text. Before you do this, take a moment to familiarise yourself with the presentation window.

## THE PROGRAM WINDOW

**The commands you will use to create your presentation are accessed via the Ribbon. Click on a tab to display buttons grouped by similar function.**

**Microsoft Office button**
*Gives options for opening, printing and saving presentations.*

**Quick Access Toolbar**
*A customisable toolbar of buttons that activate common commands such as save and print.*

**Minimise and maximise**
*When the middle button contains a square, clicking on it makes the window fill the screen. When it shows two overlapping squares, clicking on the button makes the window smaller. Click on the left button to minimise the program window to a button on the Taskbar. Click on it again to restore the window to its original size.*

**Close button**
*Click on the red box with the white cross in it to close PowerPoint.*

**Tabs**
*Click on a tab on the Ribbon to access a range of related commands.*

**Ribbon**
*Most of the commands for creating a presentation can be found on the Ribbon.*

**Slides tab**
*Holds miniature versions of all the slides in a presentation, with the current slide highlighted.*

**Group names**
*Similar commands are organised into groups on the Ribbon.*

**Slides pane**
*This is where you will work on your presentations.*

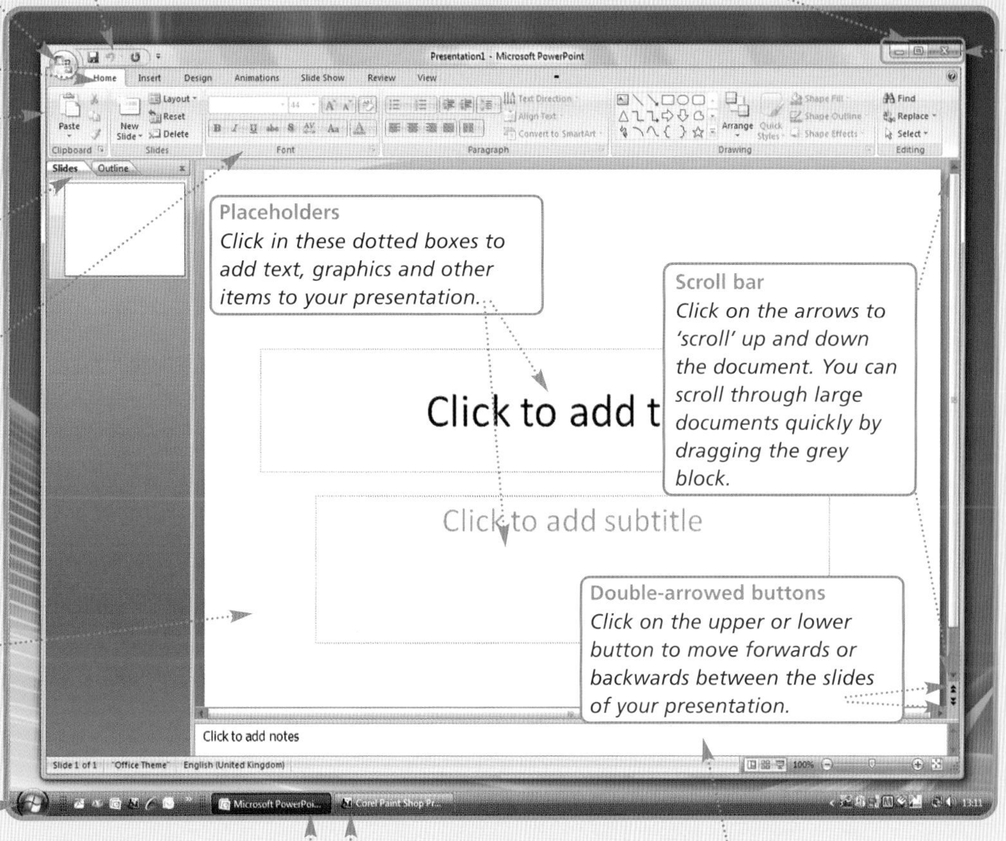

**Placeholders**
*Click in these dotted boxes to add text, graphics and other items to your presentation.*

**Scroll bar**
*Click on the arrows to 'scroll' up and down the document. You can scroll through large documents quickly by dragging the grey block.*

**Double-arrowed buttons**
*Click on the upper or lower button to move forwards or backwards between the slides of your presentation.*

**Start button**
*Click on the Start button to access your programs and shut down your computer.*

**Taskbar**
*Shows which programs/documents are currently open. A minimised window (indicated by the right arrow) is one that is running in the background.*

**Notes pane**
*You can add notes in this pane to help you when you are giving your presentation.*

# COMMAND TABS

**All the tasks you could want to perform in PowerPoint can be carried out by clicking on buttons on the Ribbon. These buttons are organised into groups and can be found under the different headings.**

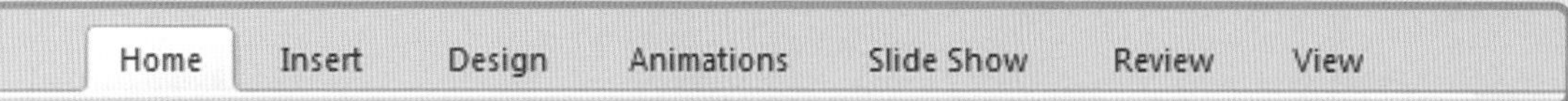


Before you start using PowerPoint, click on each tab to familiarise yourself with the options that are available. Most buttons have icons which illustrate their function.

## The Home tab

Access the basic editing, formatting and drawing functions such as changing fonts and styling text here.

## The Insert tab

This allows you to add various items to your presentation including pictures, charts and movie and sound clips.

## The Design tab

Use the pre-defined themes, combining font, colours and special effects, to style your presentation for maximum impact.

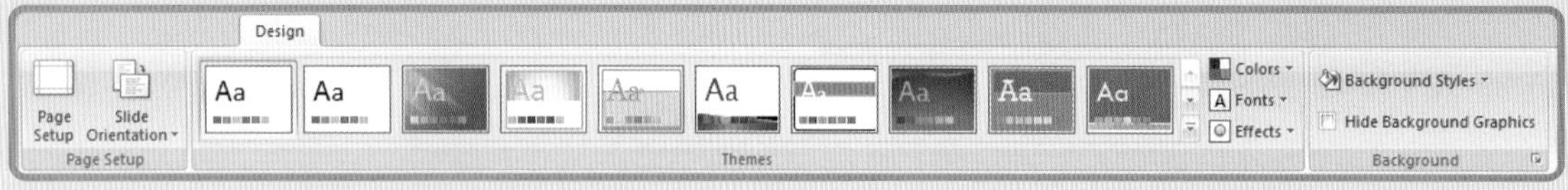


## The Animations tab

Here you can decide on how to move from slide to slide using animations and special effects.

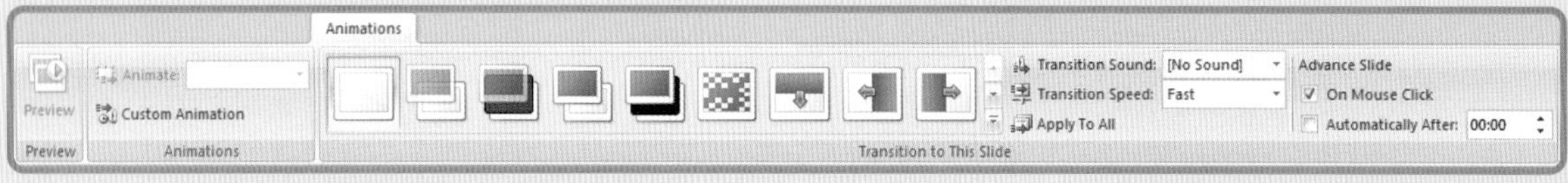


## The Quick Access Toolbar

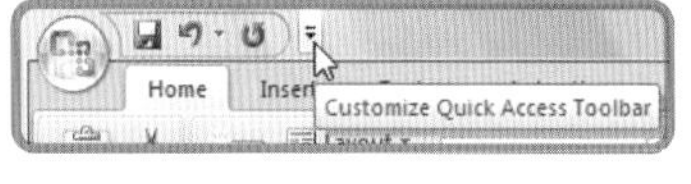


This toolbar appears in the top left corner of every window in PowerPoint 2007 and contains, by default, three commands ('Save', 'Undo' and 'Redo'), plus a button for customising the toolbar.

To add a command, click on **Customize Quick Access Toolbar** and choose a command from the list, or click on **More Commands**. In the PowerPoint Options dialogue box that appears, choose a category from the list in the left pane, then select a command, here 'Quick Print'. Click on **Add** and then on **OK**.

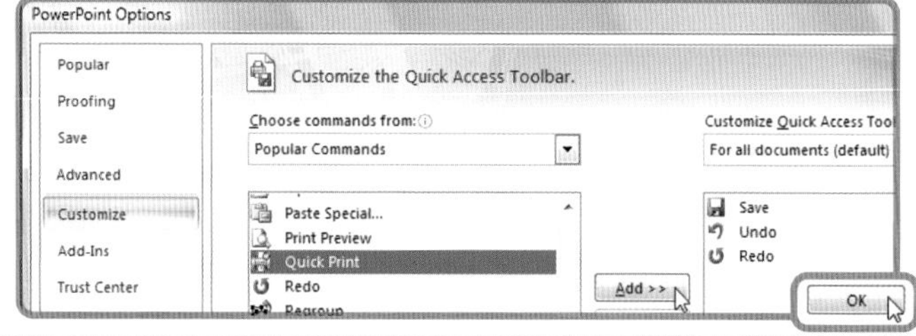

## The Slide Show tab

This tab lets you preview your slide show, make alterations to it and rehearse your timings.

## The Review tab

Add and edit comments on your presentation here and check that your spelling and grammar are correct.

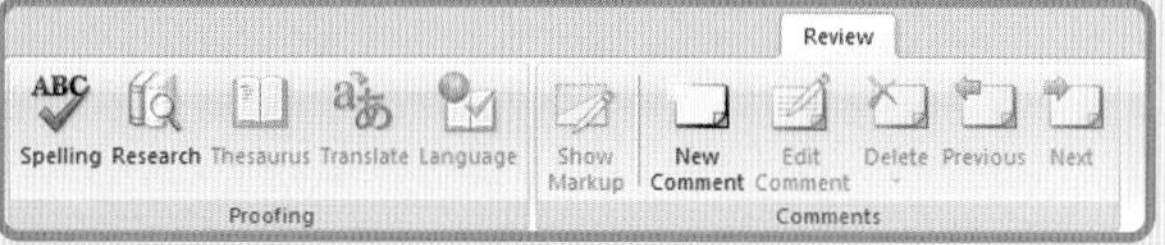


## The View tab

Here you can choose how your presentation is displayed on screen, create an extra page for your notes and see all your notes in one page.

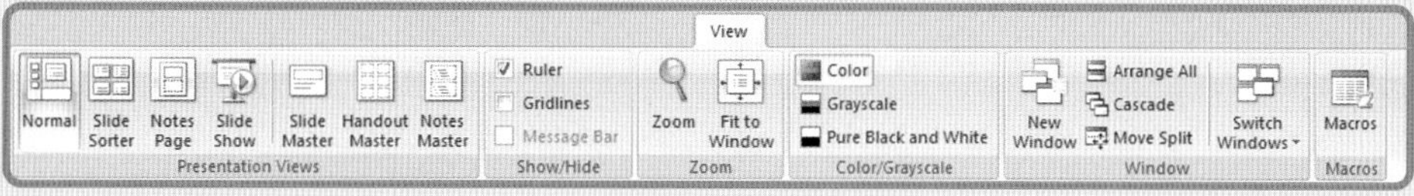


## CONTEXTUAL TABS

The tabs displayed on the Ribbon change depending on the action you are performing, and new tabs appear providing additional commands related to that action. For example, when you click on a shape the Drawing Tools contextual tab is displayed and if an image is selected in a document, the Picture Tools contextual tab appears.

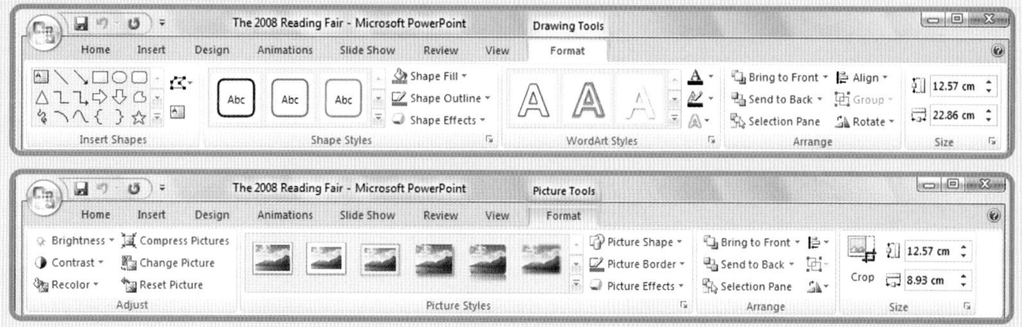


### The Mini Toolbar

Whenever you have text selected the Mini Toolbar will appear close by. It gives immediate access to the most commonly used text formatting options.

Highlight some text and, with the mouse pointer over the highlighted area, slowly move the mouse upwards. The Mini Toolbar will gradually appear over the highlighted area. Click on one of the options to style your text.

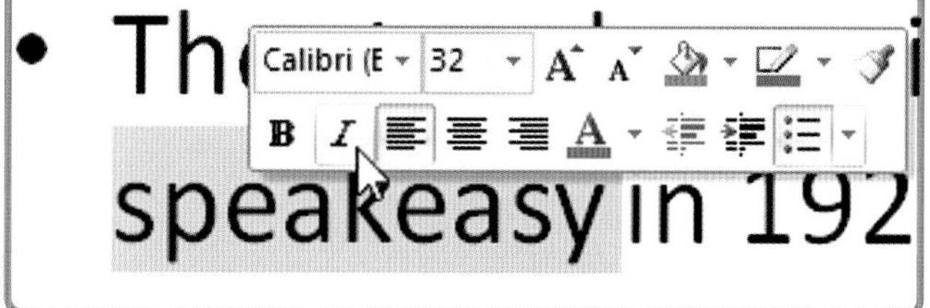

# First steps

A PowerPoint presentation is made up of slides. Think of a slide as a blank piece of paper waiting to be filled with your information and ideas. You can add and arrange content on the slides however you like, and you can make your presentation as long or as short as you want. The software gives you the chance to unleash all of your creative talents.

**SEE ALSO ...**

- *Working with slides* p30
- *Formatting text* p32
- *Arranging objects* p48

**BEFORE YOU START**

*Start up PowerPoint using either an icon shortcut on the Desktop or by locating it in the Start menu. The program automatically opens with a new blank presentation (see page 14).*

Click to add title

Click to add subtitle

The Reading Fair 2008

**1** A new presentation initially contains one slide, which you can see in the slide pane. By default, the slide contains two placeholders – in this case they are **text boxes** into which you can type a title and subtitle. To enter text, click on one of the text boxes and start typing. In the example here, the title replaces the 'Click to add title' placeholder text.

**2** When you reach the end of the first line in a text box, the text automatically flows onto a new line. You can also start a new line manually by pressing the **Return** key. The blinking text cursor will move to the beginning of the next line. To remove the line break or delete the last characters you typed, press the **Backspace** key. If you need to correct an error in the text, click with the mouse just after the last character you wish to delete and use **Backspace** to delete the preceding characters.

e Reading F

Staarts 7 J

The Reading Fair 2008

Staarts 7 June

Click to add subtitle

**Expert advice**

If you are creating a presentation with lots of slides, it's worth taking the time to work out a rough plan of the content first. Filling up a blank slide becomes a lot easier once you have a basic idea of exactly what it is you want to present. If you need to rethink later, PowerPoint's tools let you make amendments with a few clicks of the mouse.

**Key word**

***Unlike word-processing software, PowerPoint doesn't allow you to write directly onto a slide. Instead, the program uses text boxes which contain the text within frames. These boxes can be positioned anywhere on a slide.***

**3** To select an individual letter, word or line, place the cursor in front of the first character you wish to select, click the mouse button and hold it down as you drag the cursor over the rest of the text. Release the mouse button when the text you want is highlighted on a grey background. To select an entire single word, double-click on it. Press the **Backspace** key to delete the text that you have selected. To move the text, click on the highlighted section and drag your cursor to the new position. Release the mouse button to place the text there. This action is known as 'dragging and dropping'.

**4** You can style the text you have just entered in any way that you like, using the formatting options found under the Home tab in the Font group. To make the text smaller or larger, select it and click on the small arrow next to the Font Size button. This displays a drop-down menu from which you can choose a new type size. In the example shown here, 36pt type has been selected.

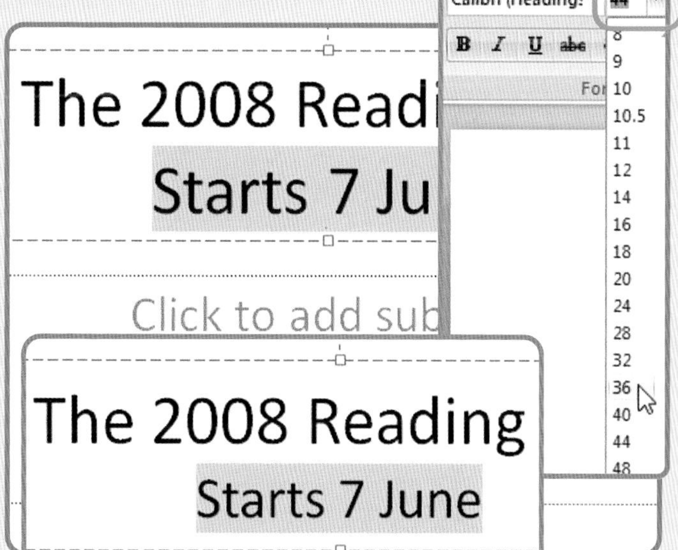

### Close-up

***There are four buttons in the Font group that can be used to style text. These are, from left to right, Bold, Italic, Underline and Shadow. Click the** Font **dialogue box launcher to view additional formatting options in the Font dialogue box (see page 33).***

### That's amazing!

You can select and highlight letters and words using your computer keyboard. Position the cursor within the text and press one of the Arrow keys while holding down the **Shift** key. The ◂ and ▸ arrows select characters to the left and right of the cursor respectively, while the ▴ and ▾ keys select all the text from the cursor to the beginning or end of the current line. Holding down the **Ctrl** and **Shift** keys in combination with either ◂ or ▸ selects all the text between the cursor and the beginning or end of the word.

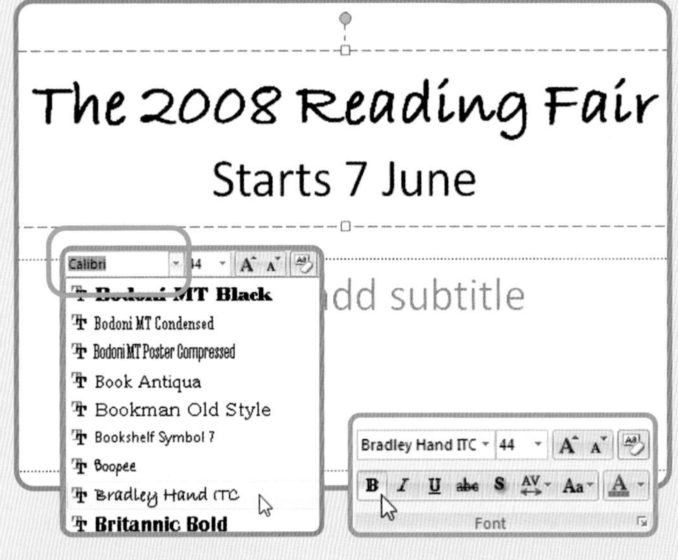


**5** When you want to change the font, highlight the text you want to format and click on the small arrow next to the Font button. The drop-down menu displays a preview of every font that is installed on your computer. Click on the font of your choice to apply it to your highlighted text. In this example, 'Bradley Hand' has been chosen. Use the buttons found in the Font group to change the font weight and style.

**6** To move a text box, click on it and move the mouse over the hatched border. When the cursor changes into a four-headed arrow, click on the edge of the box to select it and hold down the mouse button as you drag it to its new location. Release the mouse button when you have reached the new position. Alternatively, you can click on the frame with the four-headed arrow and use the Arrow keys on your keyboard to move it around.

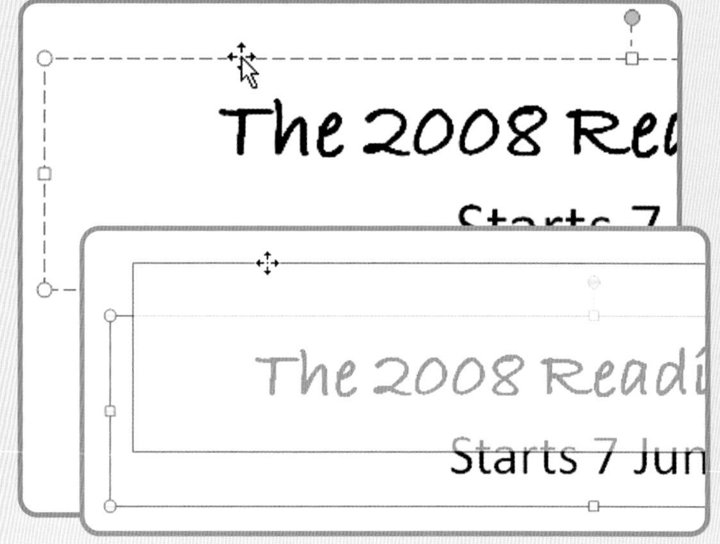

**Bright idea**

***The Increase Font Size and Decrease Font Size buttons found in the Font group provide a quick way to try out different type sizes. Use them to incrementally enlarge or reduce the size of the text you have selected.***

## Undo and Redo

Made a mistake? Click on the **Undo** button in the Quick Access Toolbar to reverse your last action. If you need to reverse that action, click the **Redo** button. To undo or redo multiple steps in one go, click the small arrow next to the respective button and select the steps you want to reverse or restore from the drop-down menu.

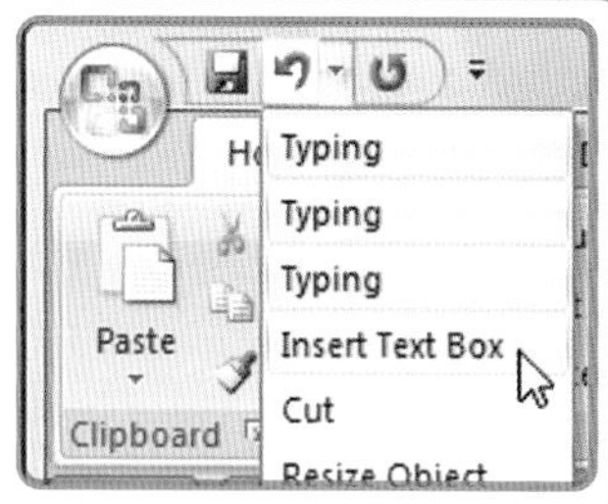


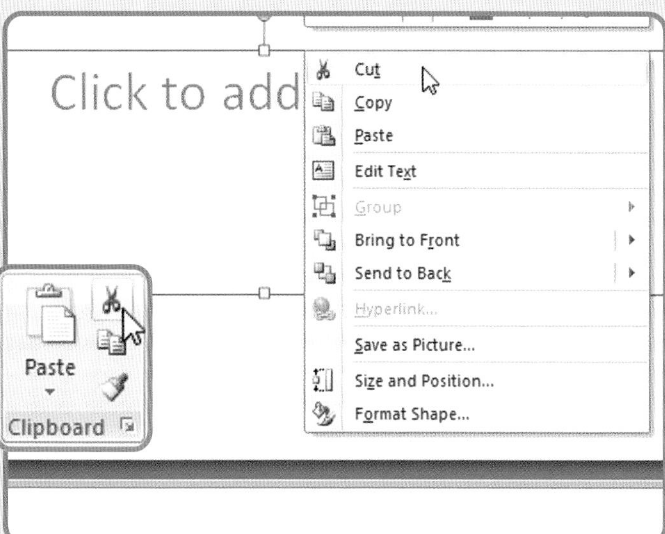


**7** To delete a text box, click with the mouse in the text box that you want to remove and move your cursor over the hatched edge. When the cursor changes into a four-headed arrow, right-click with your mouse and choose **Cut** from the pop-up menu that appears. Alternatively, you can click on the **Cut** button in the Clipboard group found under the Home tab, or press the **Backspace** or **Delete** keys on your keyboard.

**8** To create a new text box, click on the **Text Box** button in the Drawing group, found under the Home tab. The cursor will change into an inverted crucifix. Click on the slide where you want to put the text box and drag the mouse while holding down the mouse button. As you draw, the cursor changes into a crosshair. When you release the mouse button, the new text box is displayed with a hatched frame. You can now enter and format the text.

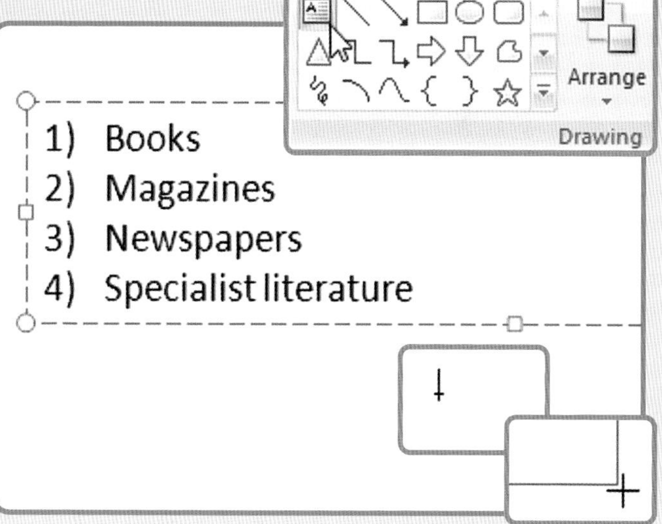

# Saving your work

Save your presentation as soon as you open a new document, and save it again at regular intervals as you work. That way, if you have to restart your machine after a power cut or computer crash – when the program stops responding – you won't lose all your work. You can simply pick up from the point at which you last saved the document.


**SEE ALSO ...**

- *Explore the program p16*
- *Creating templates p60*


**BEFORE YOU START**

*Open up PowerPoint. Click on the **Office** button and choose **New**. In the New Presentation box that appears click on **Blank Presentation** in the middle pane, then on **Create**.*

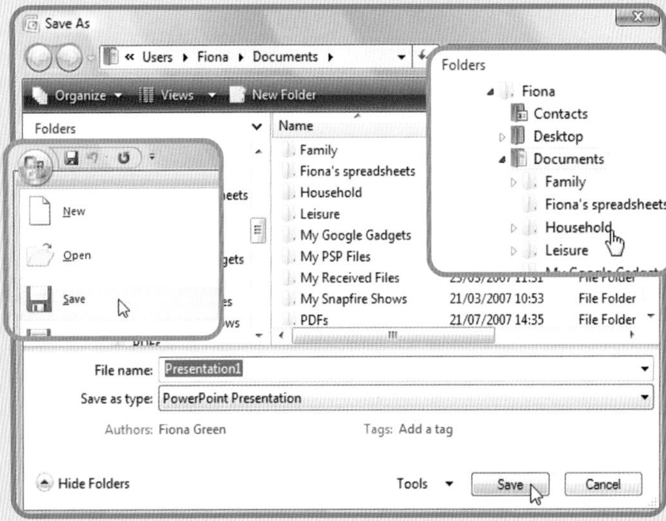


**1** To save your new document, click on the **Office** button and choose **Save**. This opens the Save As dialogue box, where you can enter a name for the presentation and choose where to save it. Double-click on the 'Presentation1' text next to 'File name' and type in a name. By default, PowerPoint will save the presentation into your 'Documents' folder. To save it in a different location, select a folder from the 'Folders' list, in the left pane. Click on **Save** to finish.

**2** Saving your documents into separate sub-folders helps to keep your work organised and easy to find again. For example, you could save presentations in one folder and letters in another. To create a new folder, click on the **New Folder** button. Enter a name for the new folder (for example, 'Presentations') and then press the **Return** key to confirm it. To open an existing folder, double-click on it. Finally, click on **Save**.

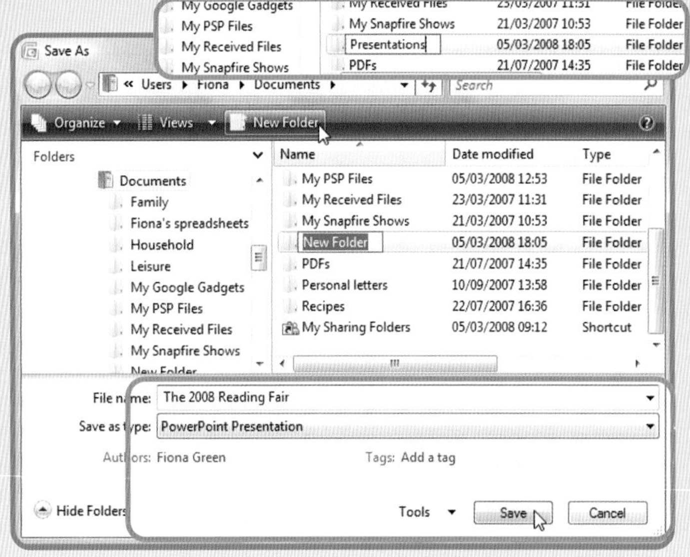

## Expert advice

To save a copy of an open document, click on the **Office** button and choose **Save As**. Enter a new name for the copy or choose another folder in which to save it. This way, you can save multiple drafts of your presentation or make a backup copy on a CD or USB memory stick.

## AutoRecover

You can program PowerPoint to save a backup copy of your work at regular intervals. If your computer crashes, you can open the backup copy from the Document Recovery task pane that will appear automatically the next time that you start the program. To activate this feature, click on the **Office** button, then on **PowerPoint Options** and select **Save** from the left pane. Under 'Save presentation' in the right pane, tick the 'Save AutoRecover information every … minutes' box and set the interval at which the program should resave the backup copy.

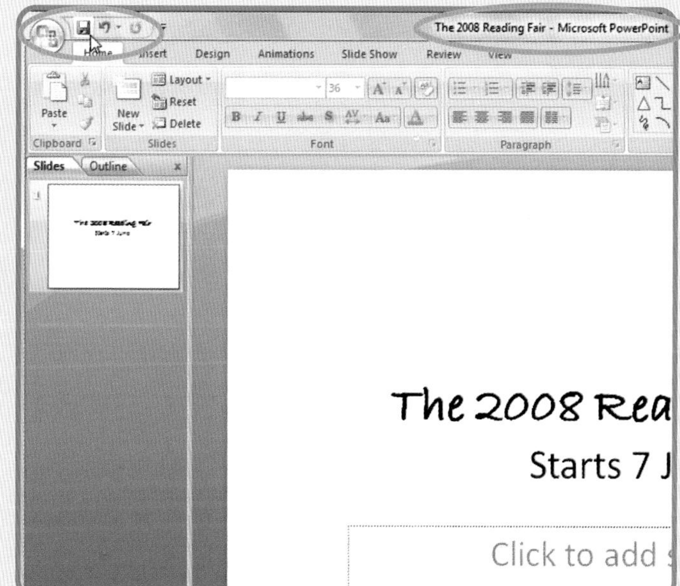


**3** Once you have saved your presentation, the file name that was entered in Step 1 is displayed in the Title bar at the top of the document window. To save any changes you make to your document while you are working, click on the **Save** button in the Quick Access Toolbar, or press **Ctrl** + **S** on your keyboard.

**4** To open a saved presentation, click on the **Office** button and then on **Open**. In the Open dialogue box that appears go to 'Folders' in the left pane and find the folder that holds your presentation. Click on the folder name to select it and then click on **Open**.

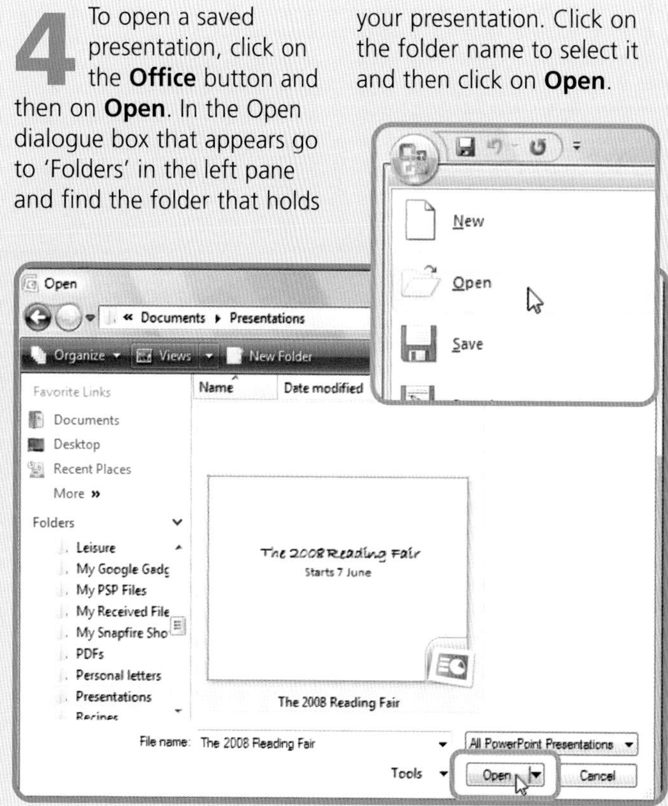

# Templates

PowerPoint 2007 comes with a host of built-in templates and pre-defined styles, known as themes, which can save you a lot of time when setting up a presentation. All you need to do is provide the content. If you have an Internet connection, you can also find a wide range of templates in Microsoft's Office Online collections, which can be downloaded and used.

**SEE ALSO ...**

- *First steps* p20
- *Presenting & printing* p28
- *Using themes* p52
- *Creating templates* p60

**BEFORE YOU START**

*Start up PowerPoint, click on the* ***Office*** *button and select* ***New****. The New Presentation dialogue box will open. On the left, there is a pane listing the available templates.*

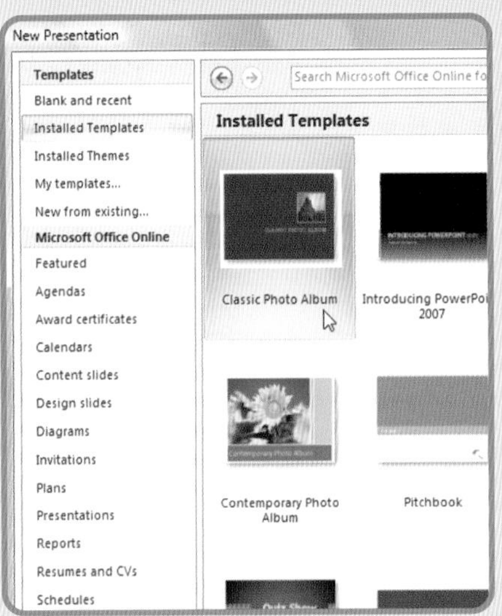


**1** To create a presentation based on one of the templates, click on **Installed Templates** in the left pane. The Installed Templates gallery shows all the templates in thumbnail size. Click on a thumbnail image to see a larger version in the right pane. Pick the one you want, then click on the **Create** button at the bottom of the screen.

**2** With your first slide selected you can now click on one of the placeholders and start to type in your own text. The Slides pane on the left of the screen displays thumbnail images of the different styles of slide available to use in your presentation.

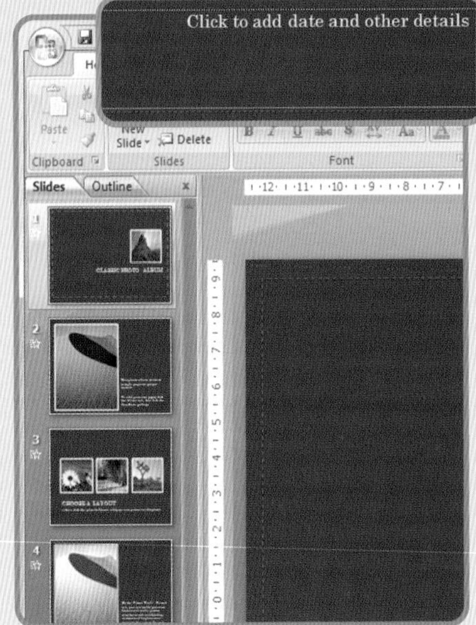


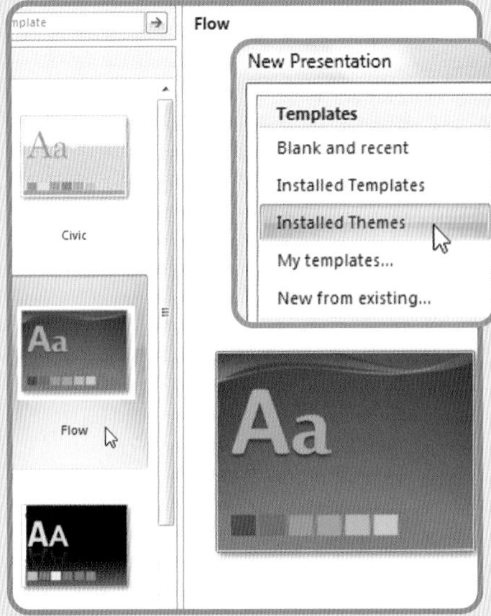


**3** Once you have selected a template, you can decide on a theme. A theme is a preset style which can be used in the design of your presentation. Click on the **Office** button, then select **New**, then **Installed Themes**. Click on a theme in the left-hand pane, and then on **Create**.

## Zooming

PowerPoint automatically selects a zoom level that allows the entire slide area to fit in the open document window. To change the zoom level, click on the current percentage displayed at the bottom of the presentation window. In the Zoom dialogue box, choose a new value from the options listed and then click on **OK**.

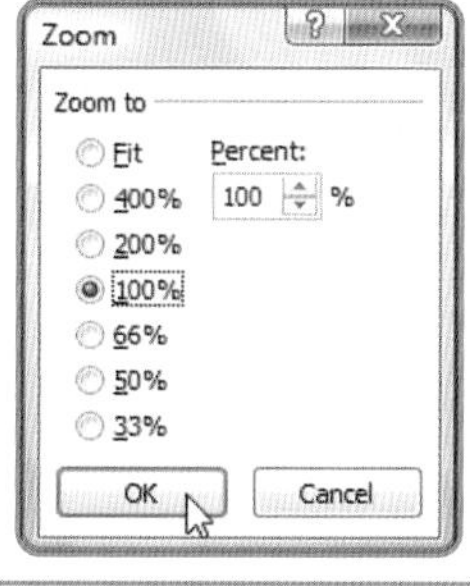


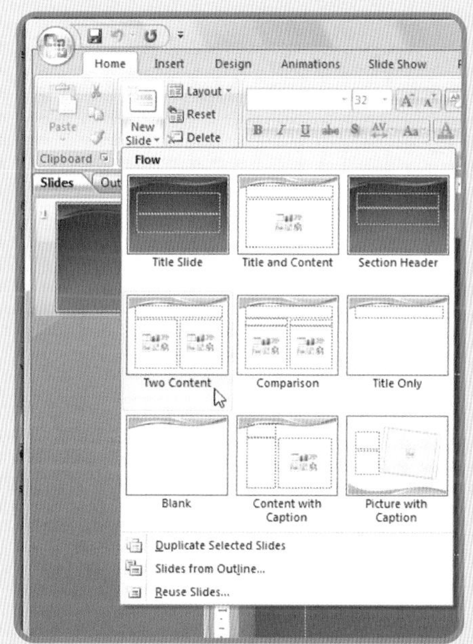


**4** Click on the **New Slide** button in the Slides group found under the Home tab. The New Slide gallery will display all of the available slide types styled in that particular theme, in this case 'Flow'.

**5** If you have an Internet connection you can access even more templates. Click on the **Office** button, select **New**, then in the Microsoft Office Online section in the left pane select a category, here **Design slides**. In the middle pane select a sub-category, click on a template, then on **Download**. A small window appears while the template downloads.

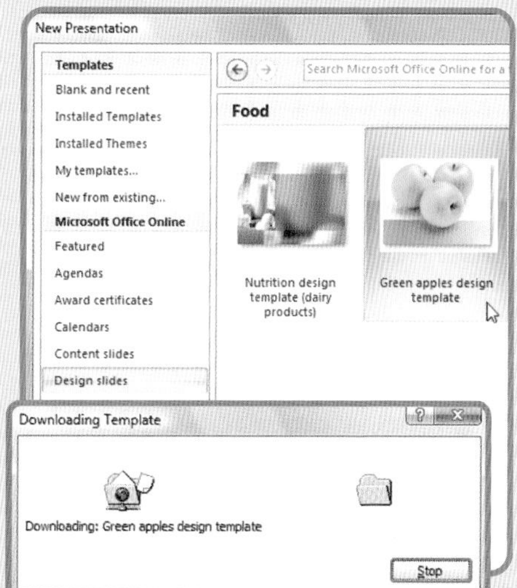


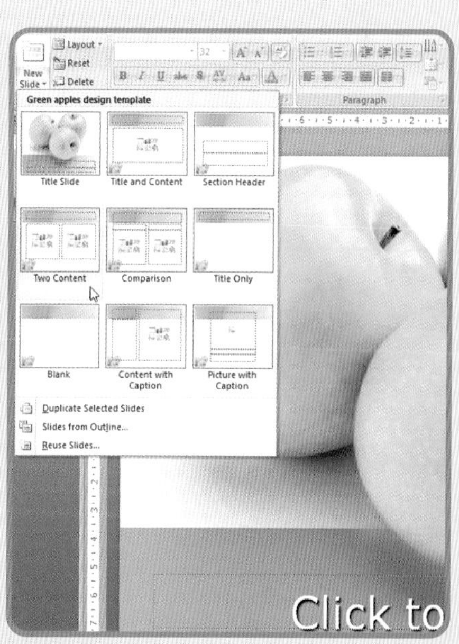


**6** The template automatically opens up a new presentation. Click on the **New Slide** button in the Slides group and the New Slide gallery will display the slide types available for that template in the background, here it is 'Green apples'.

# Presenting & printing

Creating a selection of slides is the first step towards a good presentation. The second step is to present your slides to an audience. The two most popular methods of doing this are on-screen presentations – which can either be viewed on a computer monitor or on a wall screen with the help of a projector – and presentation printouts.


**SEE ALSO ...**

- *Templates* p26
- *Print settings* p90
- *Slide shows* p92


## FLEXIBLE & SIMPLE

**In most cases, you can decide how you want to present your presentation after you have started work on it.**

### On screen

The most efficient way to give a presentation is on the computer screen itself. The individual slides are displayed full-screen in what is known as a slide show. To start the slide show, click on the **View** tab and then on **Slide Show** in the Presentation Views group. You can move through

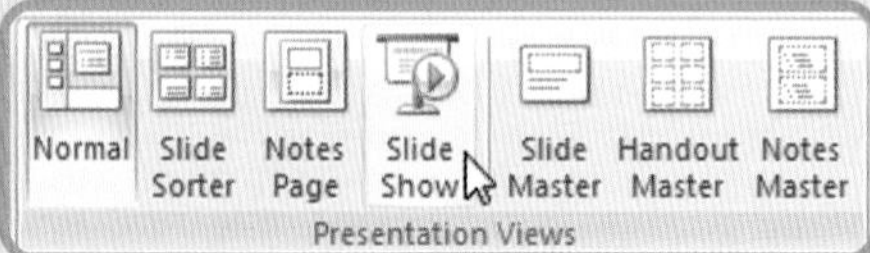


the slides using your keyboard: press the **Return**, **Spacebar** or ▸ keys to go to the next slide and use the **Backspace** or ◂ keys to view the preceding slide. To end the slide show, press the **Esc** key (see page 92).

### Printouts

Printing out your presentations is straightforward, and allows you to create handouts from your slides and produce overhead transparencies. Click on the **Office** button and select **Print** to open the Print dialogue box. There are numerous settings to choose from, and you'll find options for printing in black-and-white or colour in the 'Color/grayscale' drop-down menu. To see how your presentation will look before you print it out, click on **Preview**.

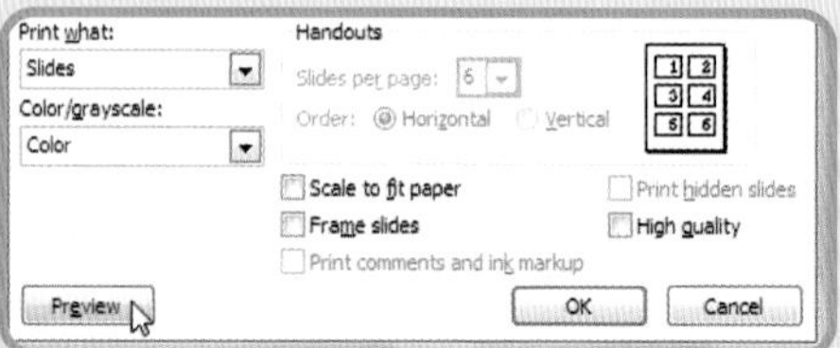


Alternatively, you can create handouts in Microsoft Office Word. Click on the **Office** button and select **Publish** in the left pane. Then click on **Create Handouts in Microsoft Office Word** in

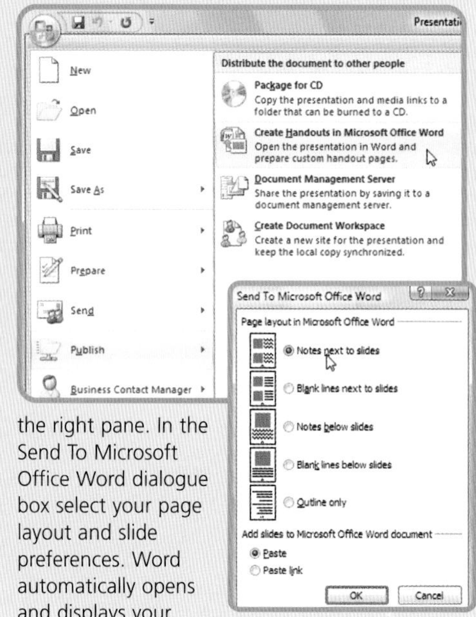


the right pane. In the Send To Microsoft Office Word dialogue box select your page layout and slide preferences. Word automatically opens and displays your slides in the format you chose.

### Expert advice

Using a digital projector to give your presentation creates a really professional impression. Link the projector up to your PC and the screen image can be projected directly onto the wall. If you plan to do this frequently, it may be worth buying a projector. Otherwise, it is more cost-effective to rent one from a photographic shop.

### That's amazing!

Some photographic laboratories can turn your PowerPoint slides into conventional 35mm slides. These allow you to present your presentation to a large audience even if you don't have a digital or overhead projector. The image quality found on the 35mm slides is superb.

# Creating your Presentation

# Working with slides

Most of the presentations you create will be longer than just one slide, so adding slides is one of the most common tasks you will perform in PowerPoint. Once you have created the right number of slides, you may find that you need to change the running order. Reordering, deleting and duplicating slides are simple operations to perform.


**SEE ALSO ...**

- *Pictures & Clip Art* p38
- *Working with Masters* p56
- *Transition effects* p84


**BEFORE YOU START**

*Open the presentation you saved in the 'Saving your work' project (page 24). Make sure that the Slides tab is visible. If it isn't, click on the* ***View*** *tab and select* ***Normal*** *in the Presentations View group.*

**1** The Slides tab on the left of the screen contains thumbnails of all the slides in your presentation (the presentation shown here only contains a title slide). To add a new slide, first select the slide after which you want the new slide to appear. Then, with the Home tab selected, click on the arrow on the New Slide button in the Slides group, or press **Ctrl** + **M** on your keyboard.

**2** When you click on the down arrow on the New Slide button the Office Theme gallery will appear. Here you can choose a layout style for your new slide from the variety of preset layout options available. Click on the layout of your choice to select it. In this example, the 'Title Only' layout has been selected.

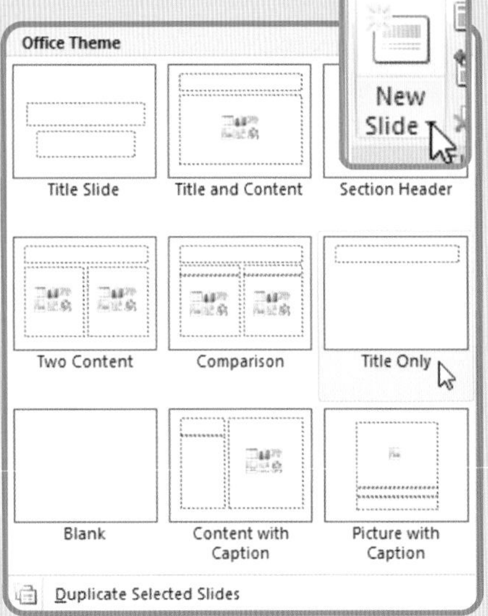


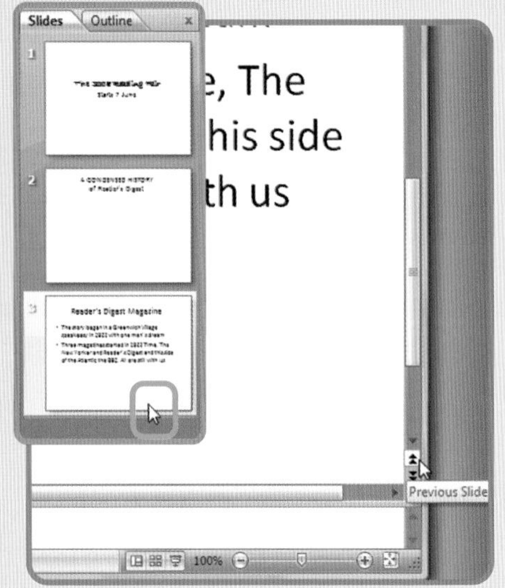


**3** In the left pane on the screen, under the Slides tab, you can move from one slide to another by clicking on the slide thumbnails. Alternatively, press the **Page Up** key on the keyboard to move to the next slide and the **Page Down** key to show the preceding slide, or click on the double-arrowed buttons in the scrollbar.

### Expert advice

If you are working on a presentation containing lots of slides, it's a good idea to switch to **Slide Sorter view**, which is found in the Presentation Views group under the View tab. Unlike Normal view – which only shows thumbnails on the left-hand side of the screen – Slide Sorter view devotes the entire window area to the slide thumbnails, allowing you to see more slides. You can also change the order of the slides in Slide Sorter view by dragging and dropping them to new positions.

### Bright idea

***To select multiple slides, click on each slide in turn while holding down the*** *Shift* ***key. You can then delete, move or duplicate all the selected slides in one go.***

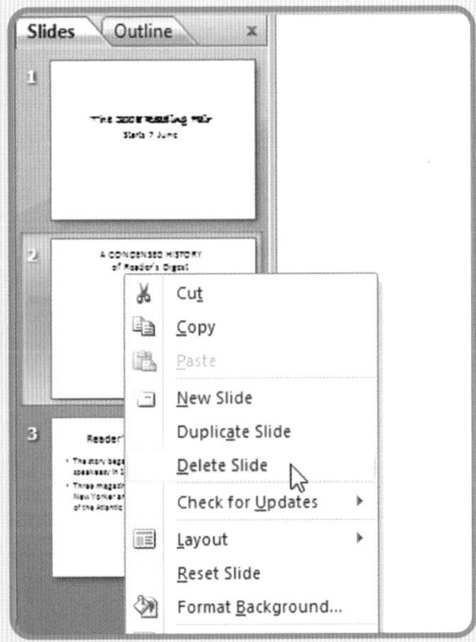


**4** To delete a slide, right-click on its thumbnail in the Slides tab and choose **Delete Slide** from the drop-down menu. You can also delete a slide by selecting its thumbnail image and pressing the **Backspace** or **Delete** keys on your keyboard.

**5** To reorder the slides in your presentation, click the thumbnail of the slide you want to move in the Slides tab and then drag and drop it in its new position. As you drag the slide, PowerPoint indicates its new position with a horizontal line.

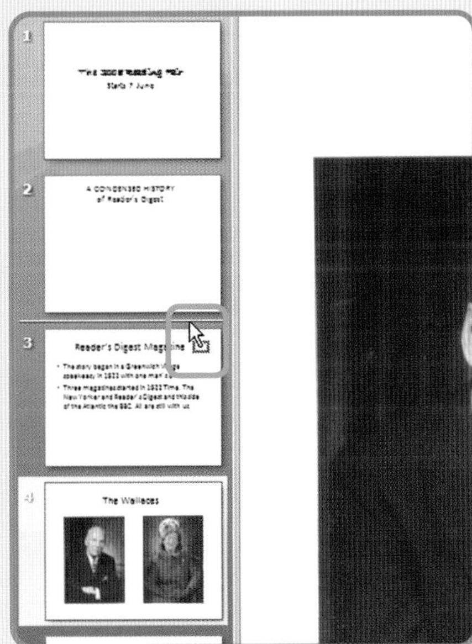


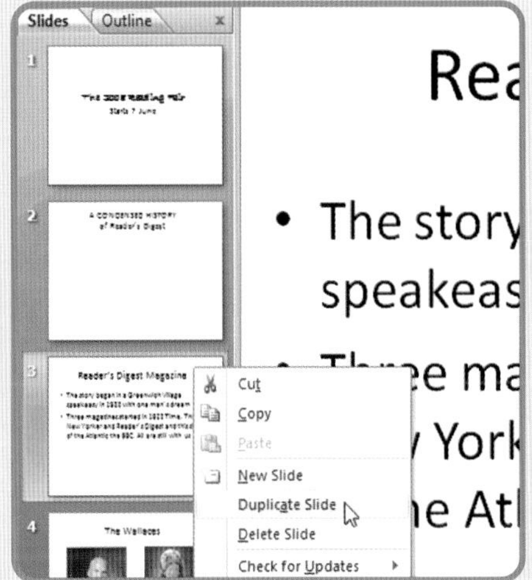


**6** PowerPoint also allows you to duplicate slides. The contents and formatting of the slide you copy are reproduced exactly and become the starting point for the new slide. Right-click on the slide you want to copy in the Slides tab and choose **Duplicate Slide** from the drop-down menu. PowerPoint inserts the duplicate slide directly below the original.

# Formatting text

Most presentations contain a lot of words, and without any formatting the text can start to look like an essay. To make your presentations more reader-friendly, try formatting the text, for example, by using different fonts and adding colour. Your efforts will pay off because it is easier to keep an audience's attention with a visually engaging presentation.

**SEE ALSO ...**

- *Using lists* p36
- *Arranging objects* p48
- *Correcting mistakes* p82

**BEFORE YOU START**

*Open up a new blank presentation and create a text box (see page 23) anywhere on the slide. Click with your mouse in the text box and key in a few lines of text.*

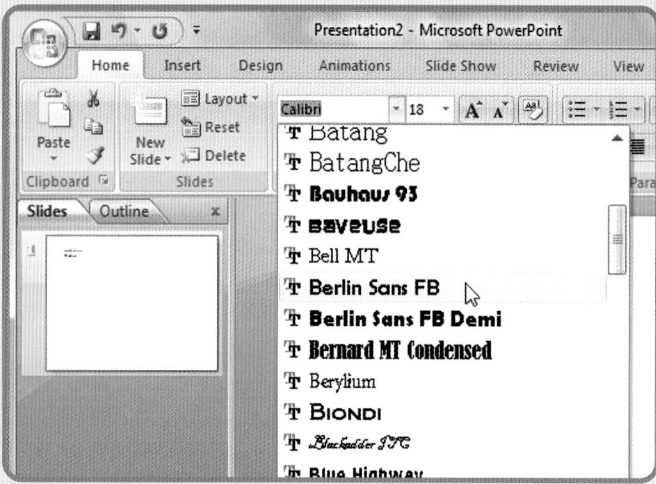


**1** To change the font of text you have already typed you need to first select the text. Position your cursor in front of the first character you want to select, then click and drag with the mouse through the rest of the text. Then, with the Home tab selected, click on the arrow to the right of the Font list in the Font group. Scroll down the list and as your mouse pointer moves over a font name your text will be displayed in that font – this feature is known as 'Live Preview' (see 'That's amazing!', opposite). Click on a font name to select it.

**2** The options in the Font group allow you to alter the font size and colour of text. You can also choose effects such as bold, italic, underline, strikethrough and shadow. To change the font size highlight the text to be changed, then click on the arrow next to the Font Size box. Select a size from the drop-down menu. To select a new colour, highlight the text, click on the arrow next to the Font Color button and select the colour from the palette.

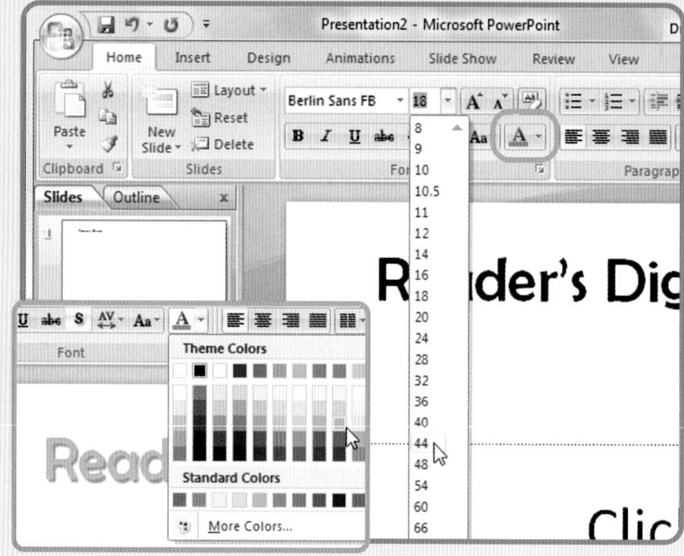

### That's amazing!

PowerPoint 2007 has a new feature called 'Live Preview'. This lets you see immediately how formatting options will affect your text before you commit to them.

### Key word

***Font sizes are measured in points (pt for short). One point is equal to 1/72 of an inch (0.352mm).***

### Watch out

Beware of using very small font sizes in on-screen presentations. At 20pt or below, type can become difficult to read – especially if you are using a digital or overhead projector.

**3** Alternatively, you can click on the **Font** dialogue box launcher in the Font group to change a font and access other formatting options. In the Font dialogue box click on the arrow to the right of the list under 'Latin text font'. Scroll down the list and click on a font name to select it. Click **OK** to confirm the new font selection. If you click **Cancel**, the original font is restored.

**4** Click on the arrow under 'Font style' and choose from the 'Italic', 'Bold' and 'Bold Italic' options. These are useful for picking out parts of the text and for making the title of the presentation clear. You can also change the font size here, by clicking on the up and down arrows in the 'Size' box. Each click either increases or decreases the size by one tenth of a **point**.

**Bright idea**

***Avoid using too many fonts in one presentation because it can become visually confusing and looks messy – two or three fonts should be enough.***

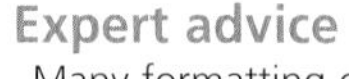

**Expert advice**

Many formatting options can be applied using their keyboard shortcuts. Press **Ctrl** + **B** to embolden the text you have selected, **Ctrl** + **I** to italicise it and **Ctrl** + **U** to underline it. To incrementally increase the font size, press **Ctrl** + **Shift** + **.**. To incrementally decrease it, press **Ctrl** + **Shift** + **,**. To clear all formatting at once, press **Ctrl** + **Spacebar**.

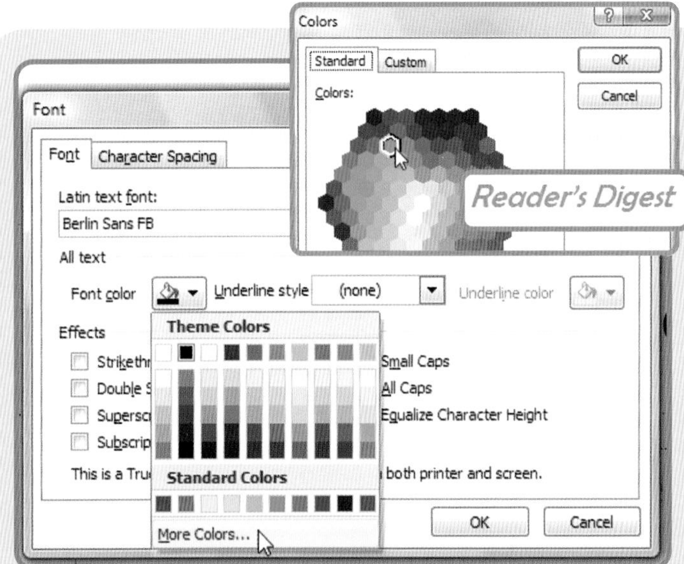


**5** To change the colour of a font, click on the arrow next to 'Font color', under 'All text' in the Font dialogue box. If you need more colours than those available under 'Theme Colors' and 'Standard Colors', click on **More Colors** and choose a colour from the colour palette in the Colors dialogue box. Click on **OK**.

Add an underline by clicking on the arrow next to 'Underline style' and selecting from the menu. Colour the underline using the 'Underline color' drop-down menu.

**6** There are more formatting options to be found under 'Effects'. Click in the box next to 'Strikethrough' to give the effect of text being scored through. The 'Superscript' and 'Subscript' options move the text above and below the baseline respectively, automatically reducing the font size in the process. Use these when creating chemical symbols or fractions. Click on **OK** when you have finished.

### Line Spacing button

Another way of adjusting line spacing within paragraphs (see Step 8), is to place your cursor in the paragraph and then, with the Home tab selected, click on the **Line Spacing** button in the Paragraph group. Scroll down the list and click on one of the preset values. To change multiple paragraphs you must highlight all the text to be changed before selecting a new value.

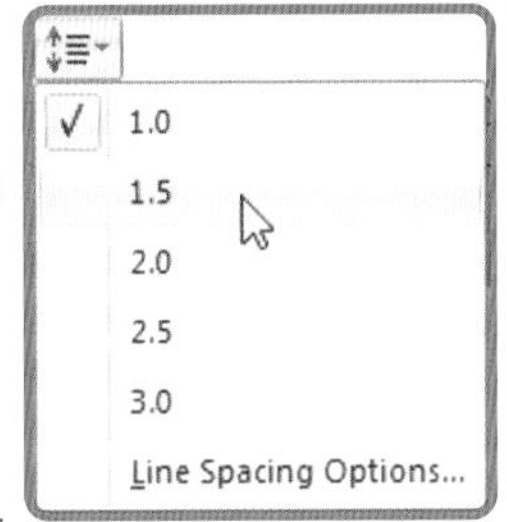

### Close-up

***In the Font drop-down menu, the fonts that you have used most frequently always appear at the top of the list under the heading 'Recently Used Fonts'. This makes finding your favourite fonts quick and easy.***

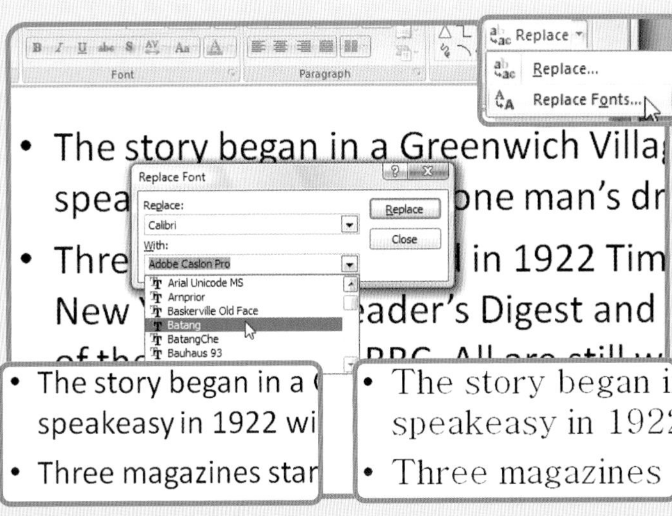


**7** PowerPoint allows you to replace every instance of a particular font used in your presentation with another font, without having to select each section of text individually. With the Home tab selected, click on the arrow next to Replace in the Editing group, and then on **Replace Fonts**. In the Replace Font dialogue box click on the arrow next to 'Replace' and select the font you want to replace. Click on the arrow next to 'With' and select a replacement font (here 'Batang'). When you click on **Replace** all text in the original font is set in 'Batang' instead.

**8** To control the space between and within paragraphs, highlight the text to be changed then, with the Home tab selected, click on the **Paragraph** dialogue box launcher. In the Paragraph dialogue box click on the down arrow next to the 'Line Spacing' box in the 'Spacing' section and select from the drop-down menu. The amount of space before and after paragraphs is specified using the 'Before' and 'After' boxes. Click **OK** to view your changes.

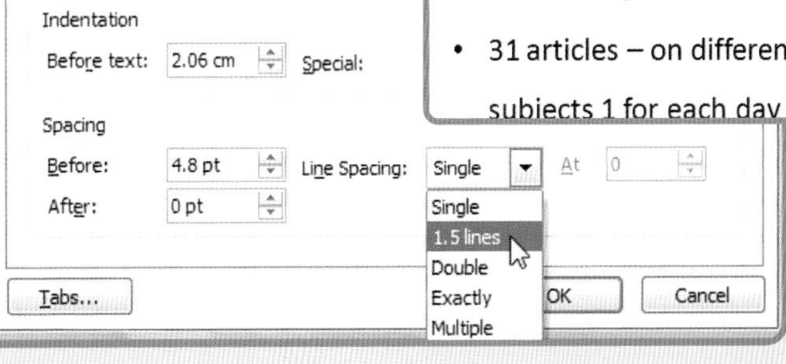

# Using lists

For your presentation to be a real success, your audience must be able to grasp what you are trying to say quickly and easily. To ensure that this happens, the text needs to be well structured and clearly laid out. Bulleted and numbered lists are an ideal way to achieve this, and they will also help you to clarify the structure of the presentation in your own mind.

**SEE ALSO ...**

- *Formatting text* p32
- *Arranging objects* p48
- *Animations* p86

## LAYING OUT TEXT

**You can either set up bulleted or numbered lists when creating a new slide, or add them later when needed.**

When creating a new slide, you can use a layout that has an in-built list function. These layouts have content placeholders with icons in them, for example 'Two Content'. Select a slide by clicking on the **New Slide** button in the Slides group found under the Home tab, or press **Ctrl** + **M** on the keyboard (see page 30). The Office Theme pane will open and you can select a layout. Click on the 'Click to add text' prompt within a placeholder and start typing. A black bullet point is inserted at the start of the first paragraph. If the paragraph runs onto a second line, PowerPoint indents the new line to align with the line above. Press **Return** and PowerPoint will start a new paragraph with a new bullet point.

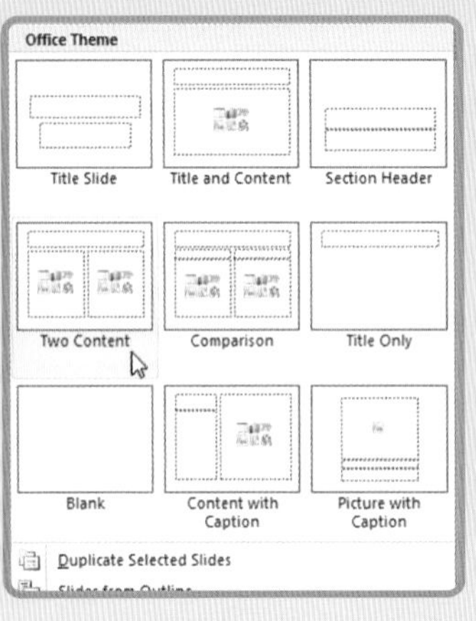


- The story began in a Greenwich Vil
  speakeasy in 1922 with one man's
- Three magazines started in 1922 Ti

### Inserting lists manually

You can insert lists into any text box (see page 23). With the Home tab selected, click on the arrow next to the Bullets button in the Paragraph group and choose an option. To create a new bullet style click on **Bullets and Numbering**. In the Bullets and Numbering dialogue box, click on the **Bulleted** tab and then on **Customize**. In the Symbol dialogue box that appears select the character you want to use and click on **OK**. Click on **OK** again to save this style.

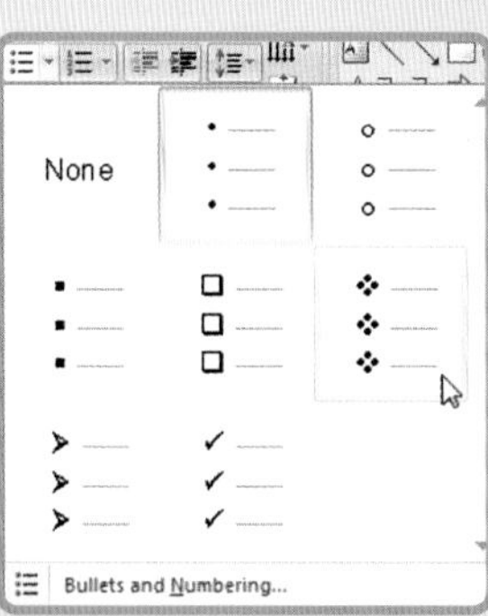


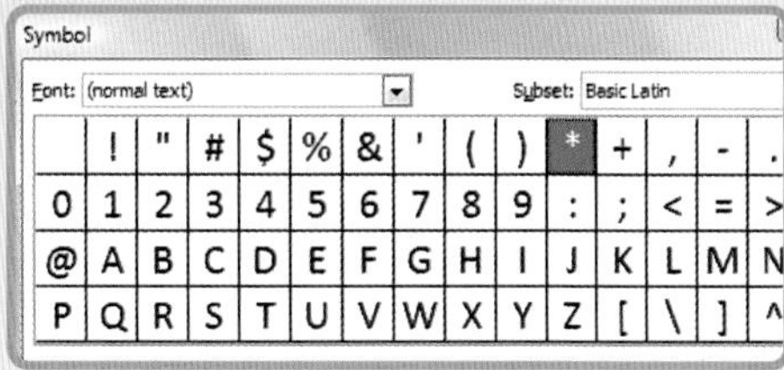


### Controlling indents

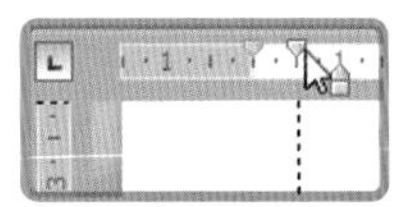

To adjust the indentation of bulleted and numbered lists, click on the **View** tab and make sure that there is a tick next to 'Ruler' in the Show/Hide group. Then click and drag on the grey indent markers on the ruler to adjust the indents. For example, moving the upper marker lets you change the position of the bullet point.

### Customising lists

You can easily change a list's appearance to match the look of the rest of your presentation. Select the items in the list you want to format and open the Bullets and Numbering dialogue box.

To change the colour of the bullet points, click on the small arrow next to 'Color' and select from the palette. To choose from a wider selection of colours, click on **More Colors** and select from the 'Standard' set. Alternatively, click on the **Custom** tab and create your own colour by adjusting the levels of red, green and blue tones. Click on **OK** to save the colour.

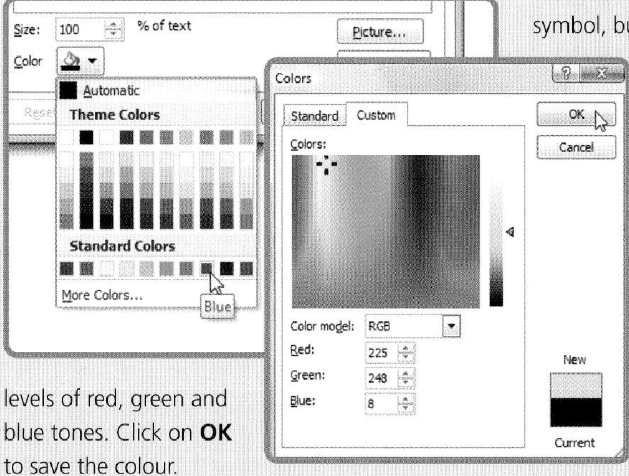


If you want to use an image as a bullet point, go to the Bullets and Numbering dialogue box and click on the **Picture** button to access more options. The Picture Bullet dialogue box will open and you can select an image to use. Click on **OK** to save your changes.

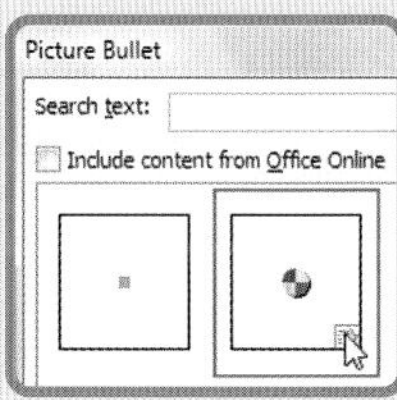


### Finishing lists

If you have finished your list and want to continue writing normal text, press the **Return** key to start a new paragraph and then press **Backspace**. This action deletes the bullet and ends the list.

## NUMBERED LISTS

**A numbered list helps to put content in order, making it easy to follow.**

A numbered list is similar to a bulleted list, except that each consecutive paragraph begins not with a symbol, but with a sequential number.

### Creating numbered lists

To add a numbered list to your presentation, click on the arrow next to the Numbering button in the Paragraph group and click on **Bullets and Numbering**. The Bullets and Numbering dialogue box opens and the Numbered tab is automatically selected. Just like the Bulleted tab, you'll find seven list styles and an option to change the colour of the list numbers or letters. In addition, the 'Start at' box lets you change the number or letter that the list starts with. Select the styles you want and then click on **OK**.

1. The story began in a Greenwi
   speakeasy in 1922 with one m
2. Three magazines started in 19

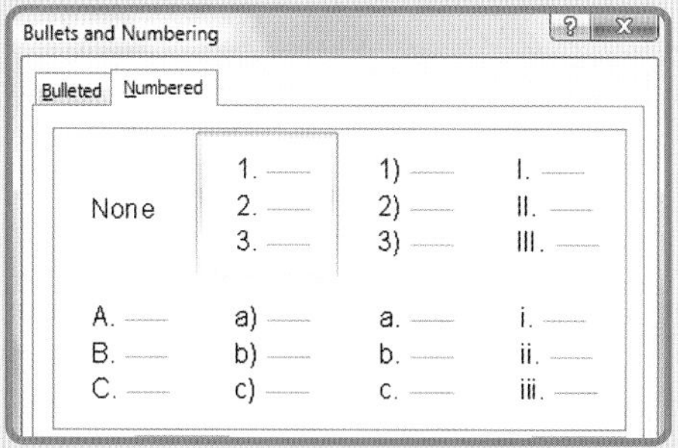


## LEVELS

**Both bulleted and numbered lists can be structured hierarchically, with up to five levels.**

To move a paragraph down one level of importance, place the cursor between the bullet point or number of the paragraph and the start of the text and press the **Tab** key. To move the paragraph back up a level, press **Shift** + **Tab**.

As you move down the levels, the indent is increased and the font size decreased. PowerPoint uses a different bullet style for each level, but numbered lists always start at '1' by default. Use the Bullets and Numbering dialogue box to change the size of the bullet or number and the level of a particular text entry.

1. Level 1
   1. Level 2
      1. Level 3
- Level 1
  1. Level 2
     ▪ Level 3

- Level 1
  – Level 2
    • Level 3
1. Level 1
   • Level 2
     a) Level 3

### Expert advice

You can start and end bulleted and numbered lists by clicking on the **Bullets** and **Numbering** buttons (not on the arrows next to the buttons) in the Paragraph group. When you create a list this way, PowerPoint produces the list using its default settings.

### Bright idea

***To turn existing paragraphs of text into a bulleted or numbered list, select the paragraphs and then click on the*** *Bullets* ***or*** *Numbering* ***buttons in the Paragraph group.***

# Pictures & Clip Art

Colourful illustrations and graphics – which are commonly known as Clip Art – provide a quick and easy way to break the monotony of a text-only presentation. It takes just a few clicks to insert and position them on your slides, and you can choose between using your own images or selecting from the graphics that come with the PowerPoint program.

**SEE ALSO ...**
- *Arranging objects* p48
- *Music & sounds* p66

**BEFORE YOU START**
*The easiest way to add a picture is to create a new slide and apply a suitable slide layout. To start a new slide, select the **Home** tab and click on **New Slide** in the Slides group.*

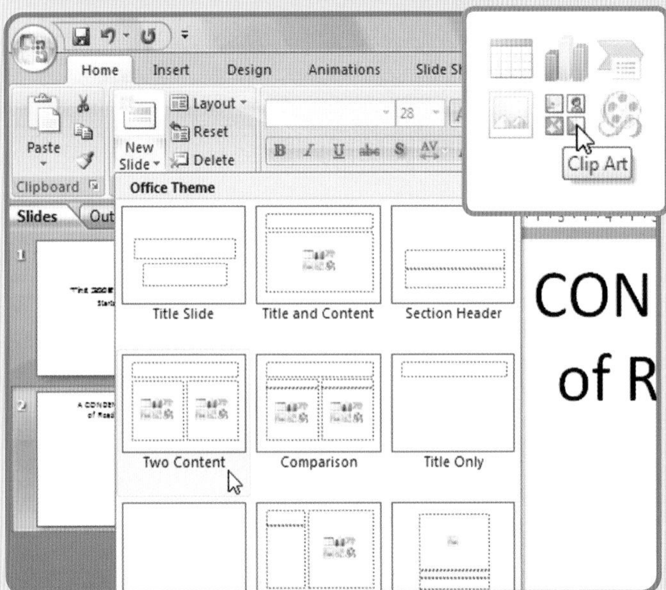


**1** In the New Slide drop-down menu choose one of the preset layouts. The content placeholders on the new slide contain six buttons which you can click on to insert objects such as Clip Art images, graphics and tables. For example, to place a Clip Art image on the new slide, click on the **Clip Art** button which is found in the middle of the bottom row of buttons.

**2** The Clip Art task pane appears on the right of your window. To search for a particular type of image, enter a keyword in the 'Search for' box. Click on the arrow next to the 'Search in' box and select from the menu the area in which you wish to search for your images. Click on **Go**. Images that match your search criteria are displayed in the bottom panel of the task pane.

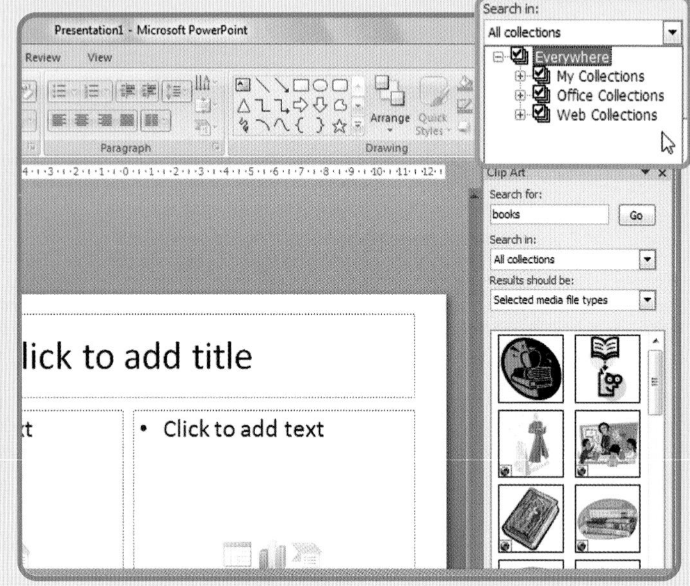

### Placeholder image buttons

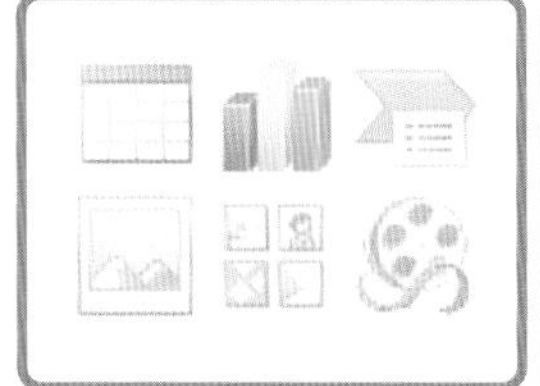

When you add a new slide to your presentation and choose 'Title and Content', 'Two Content', 'Comparison' or 'Content with Caption' from the Office Theme options, a group of six icons (in two rows of three) will appear in the middle of the placeholder. Click on these icon to quickly insert, from the first row, a table, a chart or a SmartArt graphic, and from the second row, a picture from a file, Clip Art or a media clip.

### Close-up

***Clip Art images are comprised of lines, curves and flat areas whose forms are defined by precise mathematical vectors. This means that unlike digital photos – which are formed from lots of individual pixels – you can enlarge Clip Art graphics to any size without compromising image quality.***

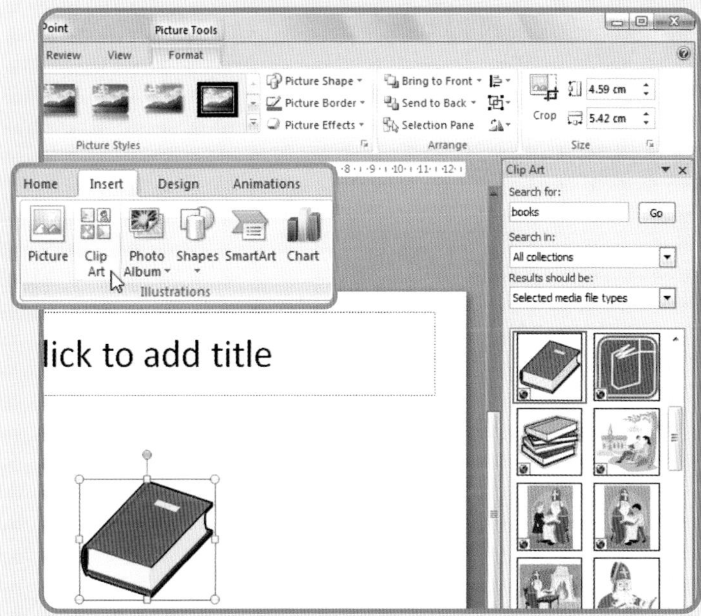


**3** To insert a Clip Art image without using a placeholder, click on the **Insert** tab, then on **Clip Art** in the Illustrations group. The Clip Art task pane will open.

Enter a suitable keyword in the 'Search for' box and click **Go**. Then click on the picture of your choice. PowerPoint will position the picture in the middle of the slide.

**4** In addition to Clip Art, you can also use your own pictures in a presentation. These must be stored either on your hard disk or on a removable disk drive. To insert a picture image without using a placeholder, click on the **Insert** tab, then on **Picture** in the Illustrations group. In the Insert Picture dialogue box select the image you want to use and click on **Insert**. PowerPoint will position the image in the middle of the slide.

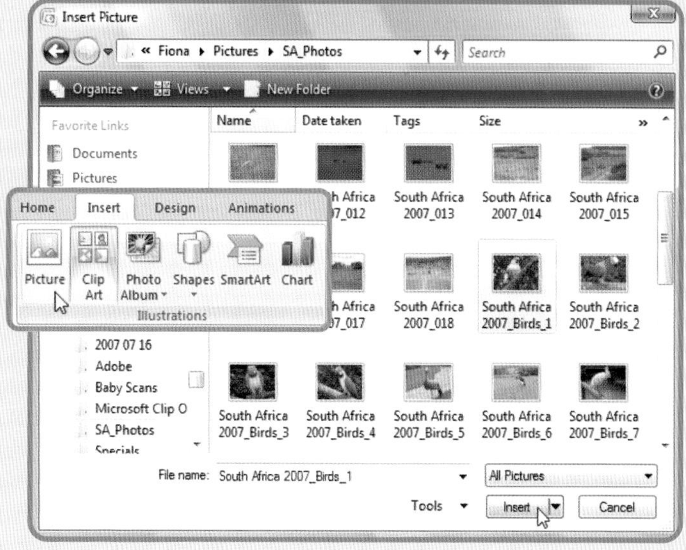

## Searching for Photos

You can use the Clip Art task pane to search Microsoft's collection of photographs. Click on the arrow next to 'Results should be', deselect 'Clip Art' and tick 'Photographs' instead. Then follow the instructions starting from Step 3 on page 39. As the pictures are downloaded from the Internet, you must be online to use this feature. It can take a few moments to insert your chosen picture, depending on the speed of your Internet connection.

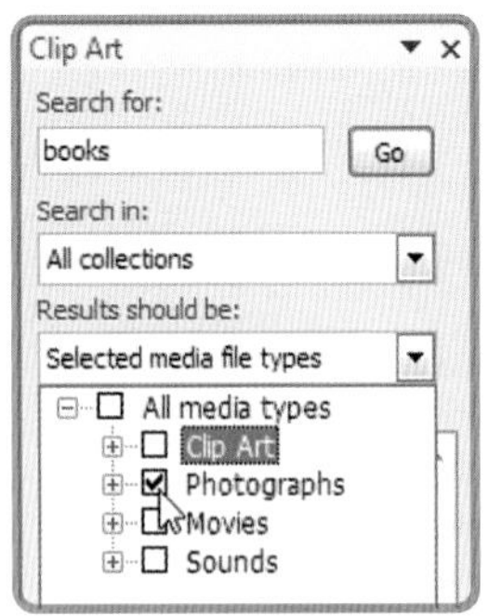


## Expert advice

When you insert pictures into your presentations, try to use images saved as JPEG files. Most digital cameras save pictures in JPEG format – it is a popular format because files can be compressed into a small size without losing image quality. You can apply additional compression to an image used in your presentation to further reduce its file size by clicking on the **Compress Pictures** button on the Picture Tools contextual ribbon.

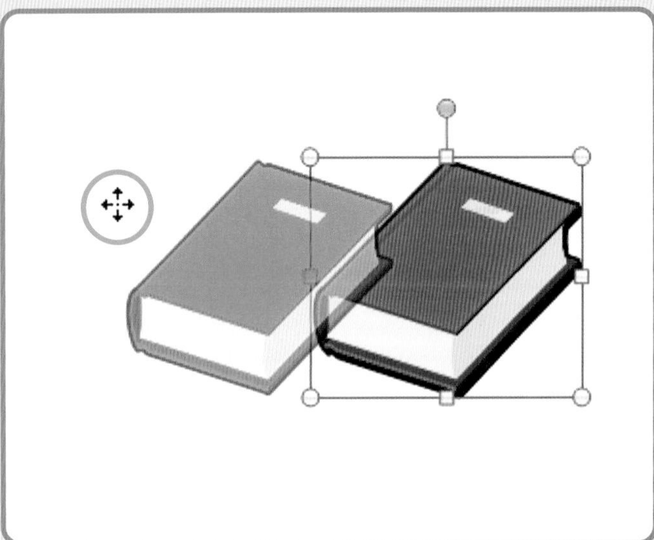

**5** The next steps are the same for all types of images. To change the position of a picture, move your cursor over the image. The cursor will change into a four-headed arrow. Click on the image and begin to drag it. As you move it, a faint replica of the image shows you where you are positioning it. Release the mouse button to drop it into place. You can also click on the picture and use the Arrow keys on the keyboard to move it.

**6** To change the size of the picture, click on the image to select it then move the cursor over one of the resizing handles at its corners or on its edges. When you place the cursor over a handle, the four-headed arrow changes into a double-headed arrow. Click the mouse again, so that the cursor turns into a crosshair, and hold down the mouse button as you enlarge or reduce the size of the picture. If you use one of the round corner handles, the image's correct proportions are maintained.

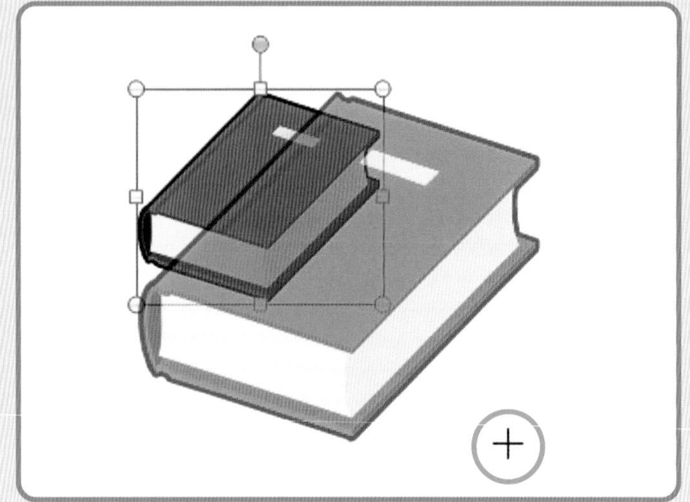

### Bright idea

***If the Picture Tools contextual ribbon is not visible, double-click on an image or on the 'Picture Tools' label on the Title bar area at the top of the screen to make it appear.***

### Watch out

The Internet has made it easy to download pictures for all sorts of purposes. In most cases, however, you may only use these images for personal projects. Using them commercially or including them in online presentations is an infringement of copyright and could result in legal proceedings against you.

**7** Double-click on an image to display the Picture Tools contextual ribbon, which will appear at the top of the screen (see 'Bright idea'). Click on the **Picture Styles** dialogue box launcher to view a range of line colour and style options, 3-D formats and image rotation options. For example, click on **Shadow** and then on the arrow next to 'Presets' and pick a Shadow effect from the menu of options. Then click on the options for colour, angle and distance. Experiment with the settings to create your desired effect. Click on **Close** to finish.

**8** You can also use the 'Brightness' and 'Contrast' options in the Adjust group to alter the colour of an image. To crop an image, click on the **Crop** button in the Size group. The sizing handles will turn into cropping handles. Hold down the mouse button and move the cropping handles until you are happy with the crop. When you want to rotate an image either clockwise or counterclockwise, click and drag the round green handle at the top of the image.

# Drawing shapes

PowerPoint allows you to put simple shapes into your presentation that will give it a distinctive look. You don't have to be a graphics expert to create them as PowerPoint's drawing tools can help you to draw shapes such as lines, arrows, squares, rectangles and circles. These can be used to highlight information or brighten up a slide.


**SEE ALSO ...**

- *Text boxes & shapes* p44
- *Arranging objects* p48
- *Organization Charts* p70


**BEFORE YOU START**

*Click on the **Office** button and select **New** in the left pane of the screen. In the middle pane click on **Blank Presentation** and then on **Create**. A new presentation will open.*

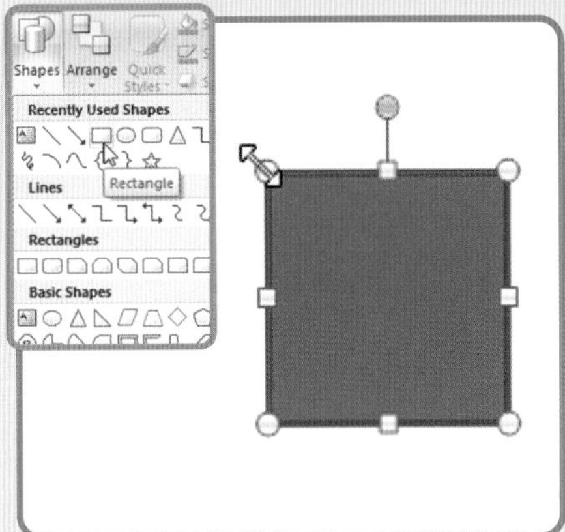


**1** To draw a rectangle, go to the Home tab on the Ribbon and select **Shapes** in the Drawing group. Click on the rectangle shape and then click with the mouse on the slide in which you want to add the shape. A standard size rectangle will be inserted onto the slide. The size can be altered.

Alternatively, click on the rectangle shape then click on the slide and hold down the mouse button as you move the mouse. If you also hold down the **Shift** key, you'll draw a perfect square.

**2** By default the rectangle is blue. To change the colour, make sure the rectangle is selected and click on the arrow next to the Shape Fill button in the Drawing group. Choose a colour or click on **More Fill Colors** to open the Colors dialogue box. Select the **Custom** tab, and click with the mouse on the palette to select a colour. Adjust the brightness using the slider. Click on **OK**.

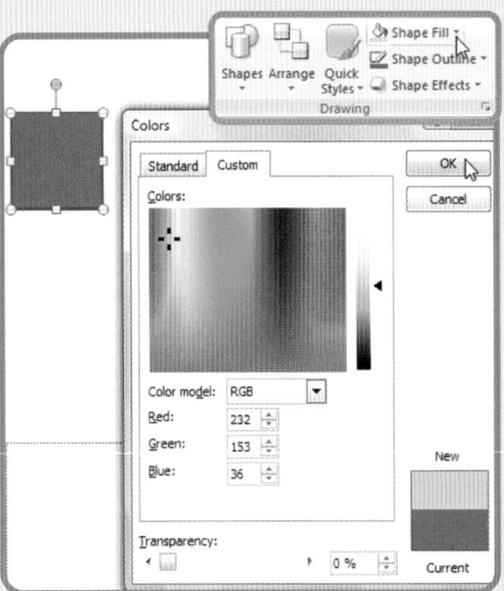


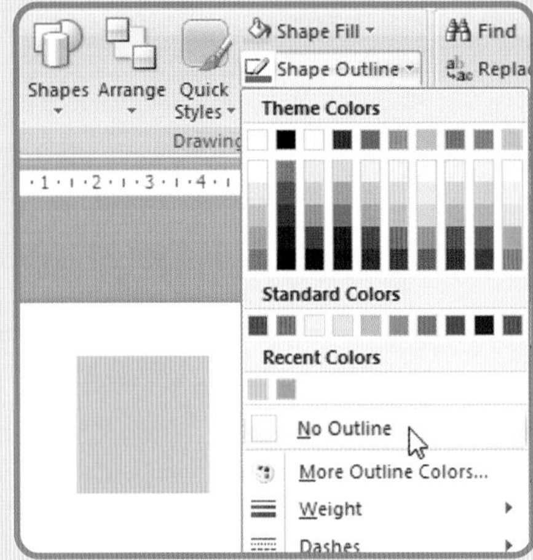


**3** The new rectangle comes with a thin blue outline. To alter the outline colour, click on the arrow next to the Shape Outline button, then click on **More Outline Colors** in the palette that opens up and choose and adjust a colour, as in Step 2. To remove the outline completely, click on **No Outline**. To make the outline thinner or thicker, click on **Weight** and choose an option from the drop-down menu.

### Bright idea

***It's a good idea to zoom in to the screen, if you need your drawing to be precise. To do this, click on the number in the box next to the Zoom slider, which is found at the bottom of the window. In the Zoom dialogue box select a higher number – for example '250%'.***

### Grouping

You can merge several objects into one unit by grouping them. Select all the shapes by clicking each one in turn while holding down the **Shift** key. Alternatively, hold down the mouse button and draw a selection box around all the objects. Then right-click and select **Group**, then **Group** again, from the drop-down menu. To ungroup the objects so that you can edit each object individually, click on the object, then right-click and select **Group** then **Ungroup**.

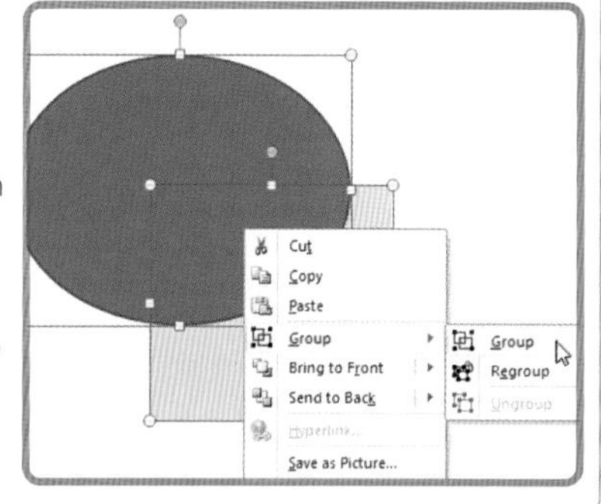


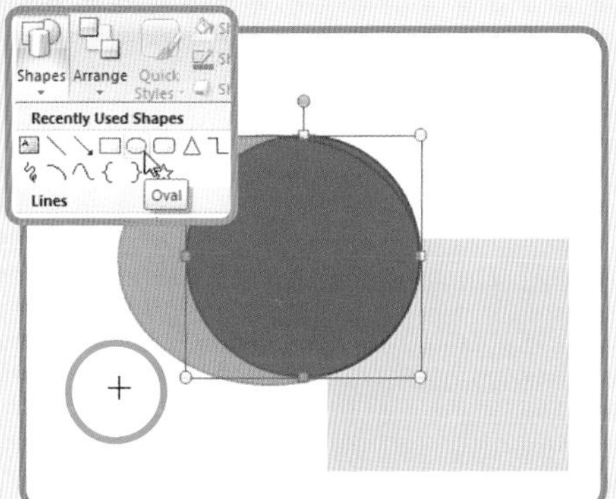


**4** Oval shapes can be drawn in the same way as rectangles. Click on **Shapes** in the Drawing group and then on **Oval**. Use the crosshair cursor to draw your shape, holding down the **Shift** key to draw a perfect circle. To resize the shape, move the cursor over a white sizing handle. When it changes to a double-headed arrow, click the mouse and drag. The cursor will change into a crosshair and a faint shape displays the new dimensions as you make the shape larger or smaller. Release the mouse button to finish.

**5** Lines and arrows can be drawn by clicking on **Shapes** in the Drawing group, then on **Line** or **Arrow**. Click and drag with the mouse to draw the line length that you require. To change the colour of the line click on the arrow next to Shape Outline. Use the same options available here if you want a dotted line or arrow. Click on **Dashes** and choose a style – here we've chosen 'Square Dot'. To change the arrow style click on **Arrows** and choose an option from the drop-down menu.

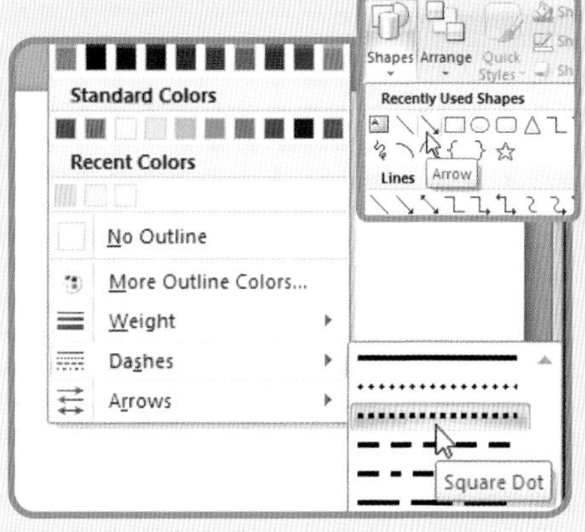


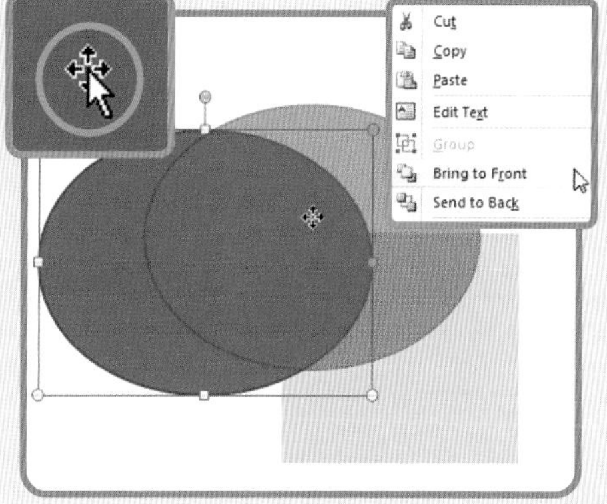


**6** To move an object, select it and your cursor will become a four-headed arrow. Click and drag using the mouse. A faint outline of the object will show you where you are placing the object. Release the mouse button when it is in the correct location.

You can put shapes on top of each other, so that one object partly or completely obscures another. To bring an object to the front, right-click on it and select **Bring to Front**. To delete an object, select it and press the **Delete** or **Backspace** key on your keyboard.

# Text boxes & shapes

There are lots of ways to make text stand out in PowerPoint. You can give your text a coloured background, apply a drop-shadow to a heading or substitute a standard rectangular text box with a more complicated PowerPoint shape such as a star or speech bubble. It is this kind of extra detail that is sure to catch the audience's eye.

**SEE ALSO ...**
- *First steps p20*
- *Formatting text p32*
- *Arranging objects p48*

**BEFORE YOU START**
*Enter some text on a slide. It doesn't matter whether you create a text box manually or use a placeholder that is already there – PowerPoint treats them both the same.*

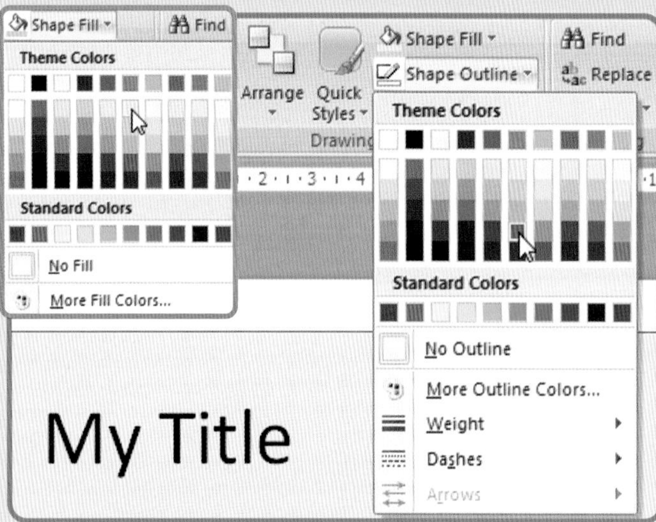


**1** To add a colour to text boxes and placeholders, select one and, with the Home tab selected, click on the arrow next to Shape Fill in the Drawing group. Select from the palette of colours under 'Theme Colors' or 'Standard Colors', or click on **More Fill Colors** to choose from a wider selection of colours. You can add a coloured border to the box by clicking on the arrow on the Shape Outline button in the Drawing group and choosing a colour in the same way as for 'Shape Fill'.

**2** To create a background with a colour gradient for your text box or placeholder, click on the arrow next to Shape Fill in the Drawing group and select **Gradient** from the drop-down menu. Then select from the options under 'Variations' – here we've chosen 'From Center'. For more options click on **More Gradients**.

You can also use one of PowerPoint's pre-set textures for your background. From the 'Shape Fill' drop-down menu click on **Texture** and choose from the palette of textures.

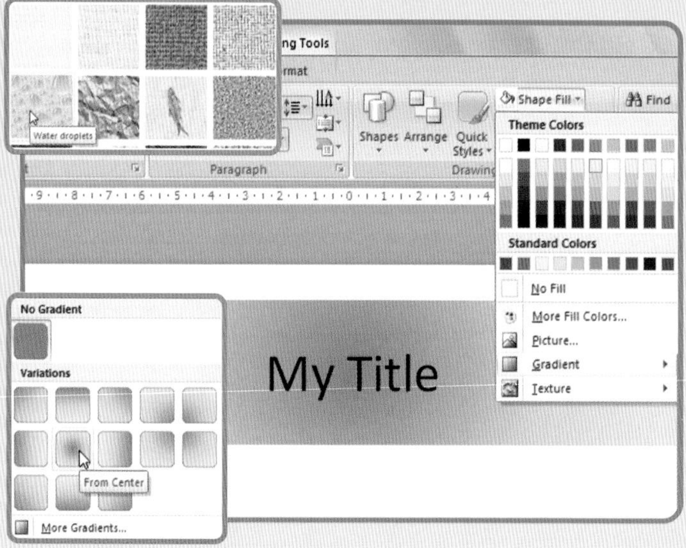

### Watch out

Using colours can greatly enhance your presentations but don't overdo it. If you use too many colours your presentation will look cluttered and messy, making it much harder for your audience to focus on the content.

### Line breaks

By default, PowerPoint wraps text onto a new line as soon as it reaches the edge of the text box or shape in which it is contained. If necessary, the program also adjusts the height of a text box or shape to prevent text overrunning its borders (see illustration top right). You can turn off both settings by clicking on the **AutoFit Options** button at the bottom left of your text box (see illustration right). To manually force text to flow onto a new line, press **Shift** + **Return** on your keyboard. This feature doesn't work in 'title' or 'subtitle' placeholders.

Here is some text that is going to fill up my text box and then hopefully reduce in size as there is too much to fit at the default size

AutoFit Text to Placeholder
Stop Fitting Text to This Placeholder
Control AutoCorrect Options...

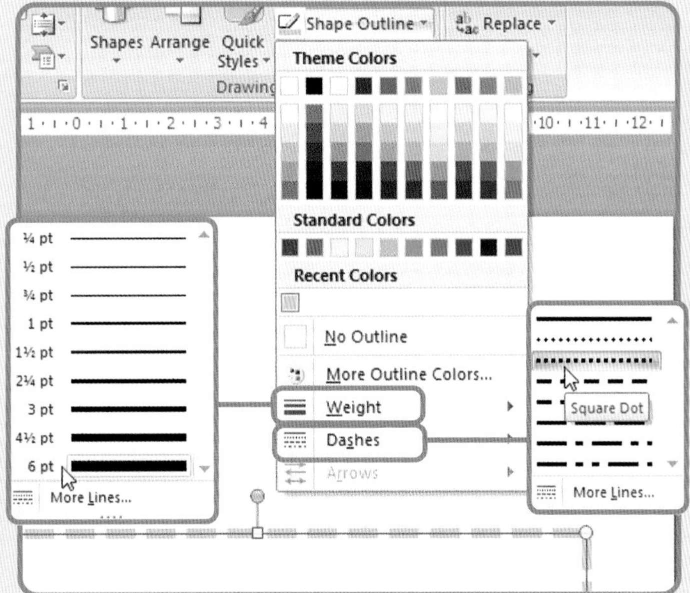


**3** You can also change the weight and style of a text box's outline. In the Drawing group, click on the arrow next to Shape Outline to display options for 'Weight' and 'Dashes'. These two drop-down menus allow you to adjust the settings for the thickness of the outline and decide whether it has a solid or broken line.

**4** You can set the height and width of your text box to the nearest millimetre. To do this, select a text box and click on the **Format** tab of the Drawing Tools contextual ribbon. Then click on the **Size** dialogue box launcher and change the measurements found in the Size tab. You can also set the box position by selecting the Position tab. The drop-down menus in the 'From' boxes allow you to set the object's co-ordinates either from the 'Top Left Corner' of the slide or from its 'Center' point. Click **Close** to confirm your changes.

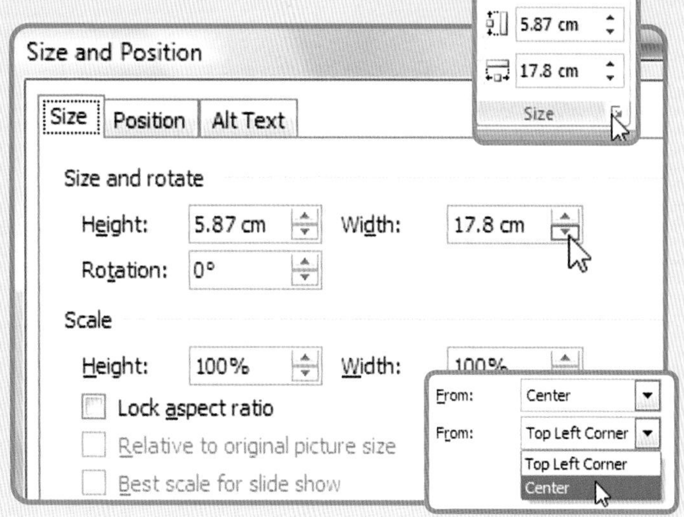

## Expert advice

You can access the 'Shapes' command in several different ways: including in the Drawing group found under the Home tab, in the Illustrations group found under the Insert tab or in the Drawing Tools contextual ribbon which appears when you double-click on an object.

## Key word

***PowerPoint's Shapes are preset shapes such as triangles, arrows and stars which you can draw by clicking on an object in the Shapes gallery and then clicking and dragging on a slide in your presentation to draw the shape.***

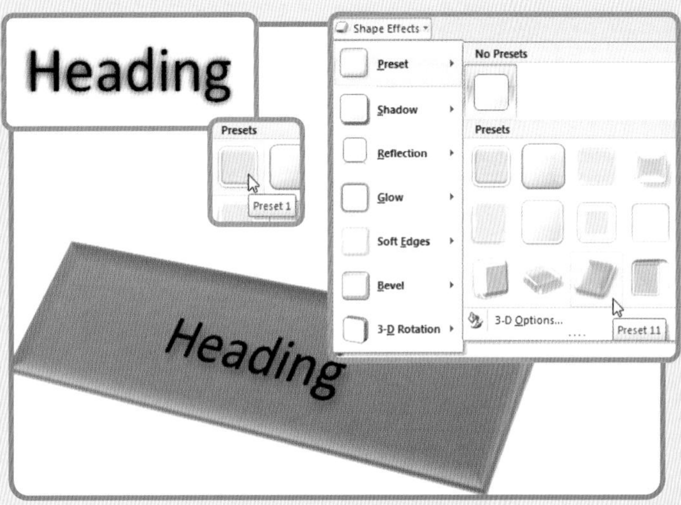


**5** The Drawing group has many options for introducing special effects such as shadow, reflection or bevelled edges to enhance text boxes. Click on **Shape Effects** in the Drawing group, then on **Preset** and select **Preset 1** to add a shadow to your text. Click on **Preset 11** to apply a shadow and add a background colour, bevelled edges and a 3-D Rotation. Experiment to see the effects. If you don't like the preset options, select from 'Shadow', 'Reflection', 'Glow', 'Soft Edges', 'Bevel' and '3-D Rotation' to create your own effect.

**6** It is possible to enter text into many of the preset shapes. With the Home tab selected, click on **Shapes** in the Drawing group, choose a category from the menu (here, 'Stars and Banners') and choose a shape (here, 'Explosion 2'). The cursor turns into a crosshair. Click and drag on the slide to draw the shape at the required size. Release the mouse button to finish. Ensure the shape is selected and enter your text.

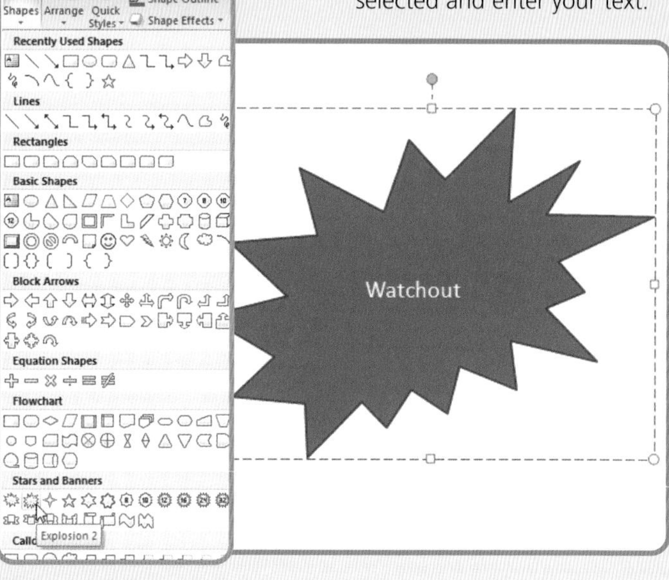

### Bright idea

***You can draw all sorts of lines and curves using the options under 'Lines' in the Shapes gallery. In addition, the 'Connectors' options let you draw connecting lines between individual shapes. These are very useful if you are creating flow charts or schematic diagrams.***

### Resizing and adjusting shapes

You can resize or adjust any shape that you have created by using the handles that appear when a shape is selected. The green circle handle lets you rotate the shape, the pale blue corner circles allow you to resize both the depth and width of a shape and the pale blue square at the sides allows you to adjust the depth and width of a shape separately. Additionally, there may be yellow diamond shaped handles, which are used to adjust the points of a shape. Here, they could be used to change the angle of the segment without distorting the shape.

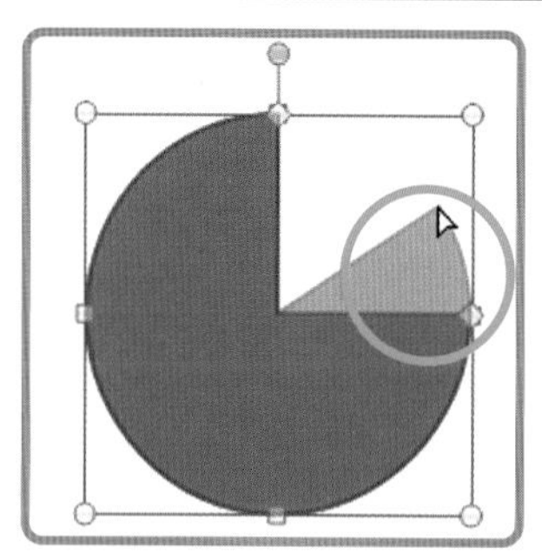

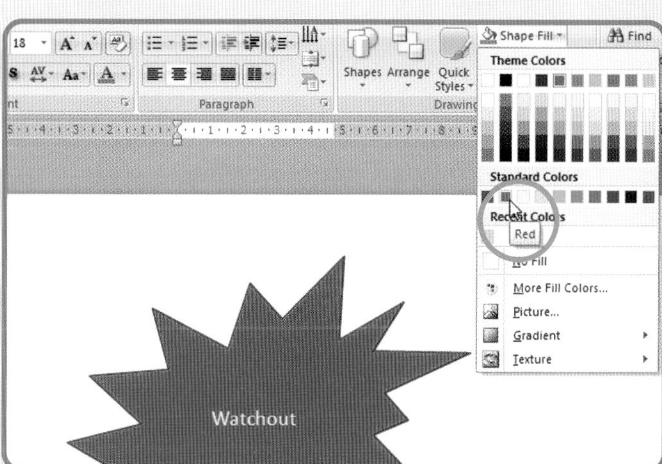


**7** You can format shapes in the same way that you format text boxes. Select the shape then, with the Home tab selected, click on the arrow on the Shape Fill button in the Drawing group and select a new colour. Now click on the arrow on the Shape Outline button and then on **No Outline** to remove the outline. Moving a shape around the slide or changing its size also works in the same way as moving and resizing a text box. To resize a shape, click on it and then click and drag on one of the sizing handles. To maintain its proportions, hold down the **Shift** key as you drag one of the corner sizing handles.

**8** Rotate a shape by selecting the object and placing the cursor on the green rotating handle found at the top centre of the object. When a circular arrow appears, click and drag the handle in the direction of rotation. A faint outline indicates the new position of the shape. For more options, click on the **Format** tab of the Drawing Tools contextual ribbon, then on **Rotate** in the Arrange group. Click on **More Rotation Options**. In the dialogue box that appears, select the **Size** tab and click on the arrows next to 'Rotation' to set an exact degree of rotation. Click on **Close**.

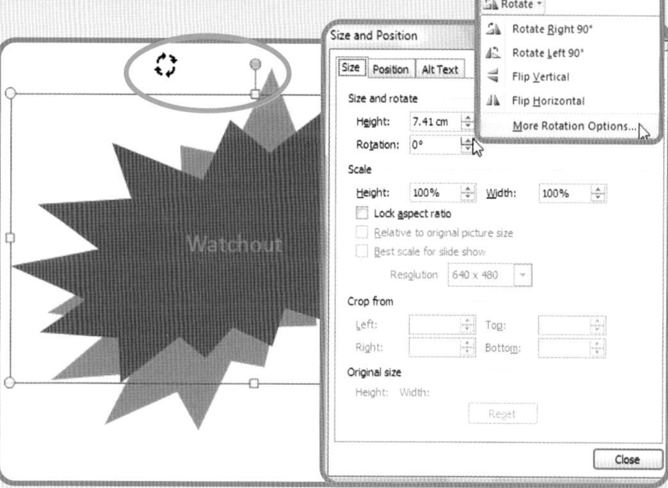

# Arranging objects

You can place any object – a text box, a shape or picture – anywhere you like on a slide. Positioning objects often requires an eye for detail, particularly if you are working with a group of shapes or pictures, but PowerPoint's tools can help. It has rulers, grids and guides that allow you to accurately align objects to the frame and also to other objects.

**SEE ALSO ...**


- *Pictures & Clip Art* p38
- *Text boxes & shapes* p44
- *Inserting charts* p64


**BEFORE YOU START**

*Open a presentation and make sure that the rulers to the left and top of the slide are displayed. If they are not, click on the **View** tab and tick 'Ruler'. The rulers will now be visible.*

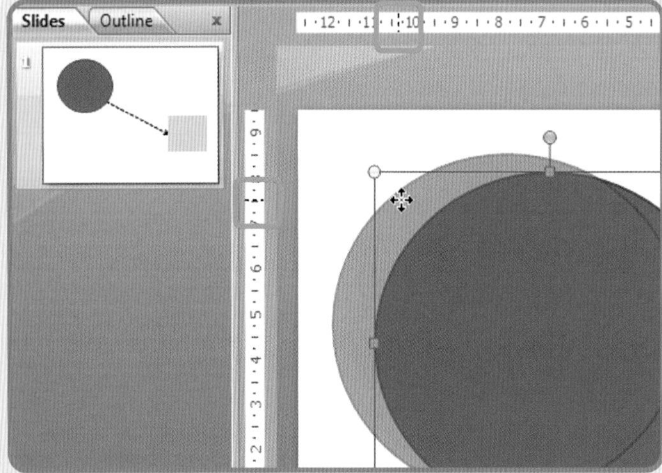


**1** Centimetres are the unit of measurement on the rulers that are found on the top of the slide and down the left-hand side. The measurements on the horizontal and vertical rulers start from the middle of the slide, and a small dashed line indicates the position of the cursor on the slide. When you use the four-headed arrow to move an object, the two dashed lines mark the position of its top left corner. By default, PowerPoint moves objects along a grid. The gridlines are 2mm apart, and objects 'snap' to the nearest gridline like a magnet.

**2** To change the grid spacing, select the object, click on the **Format** tab in the Drawing Tools contextual ribbon, then click on **Align** in the Arrange group. Scroll down the list and click on **Grid Settings**. In the Grid and Guides dialogue box that appears, click on the down arrow next to 'Spacing' and select an option – '2 grids per cm', for example, will display a grid line every 0.5cm. To prevent objects snapping to the grid, you should untick the 'Snap objects to grid' check box.

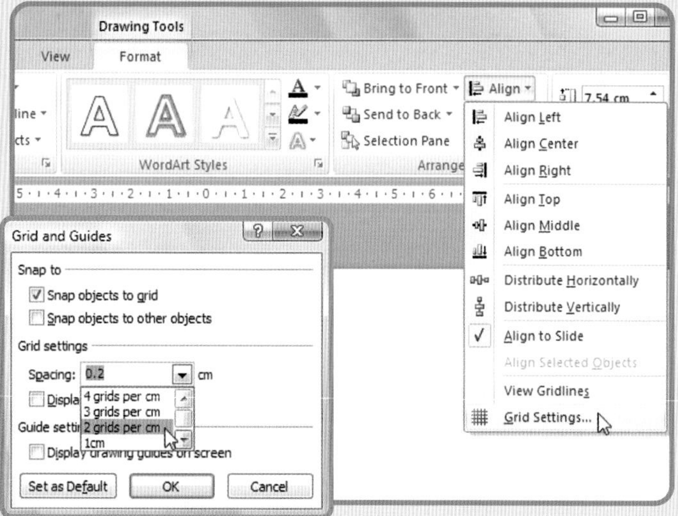

**Bright idea**

***If the grid is switched on, it is possible to position objects without snapping to it – just like you can with drawing guides. To do so, simply hold down the*** *Alt* ***key as you move an object.***

**That's amazing!**

To create a new drawing guide, click on an existing one, hold down the **Ctrl** key, and click and drag with the mouse as you position a new line wherever you want it. You can copy objects in exactly the same way.

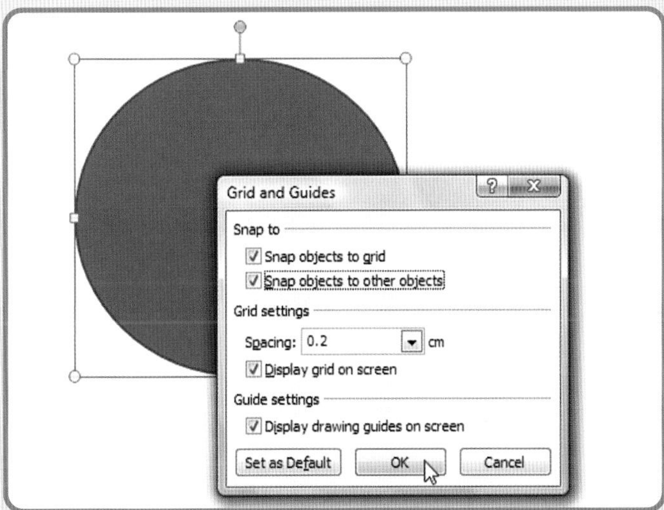


**3** There are a few other helpful features you can activate in the Grid and Guides dialogue box. Tick the 'Snap objects to other objects' box and objects will automatically align to each other's edges when moved. If you turn on the 'Display grid on screen' option, PowerPoint shows dotted grid lines every 2cm. Tick the 'Display drawing guides on screen' box and two additional guides will be displayed to help you to position objects. When you have made your choices, click on **OK**.

**4** Like the grid, guides and drawing guides act like magnets so they are perfect for aligning objects. By default, the drawing guides intersect in the middle of the slide. To move one of the lines, click it and hold down the mouse button as you drag it to its new position. As you drag, PowerPoint shows the guide's current co-ordinate alongside a small arrow (you can hold down the **Shift** key to show the distance from the guide's previous position instead). If the grid is turned on, the drawing guides snap to it. Hold down the **Alt** key to position the drawing lines independently of the grid.

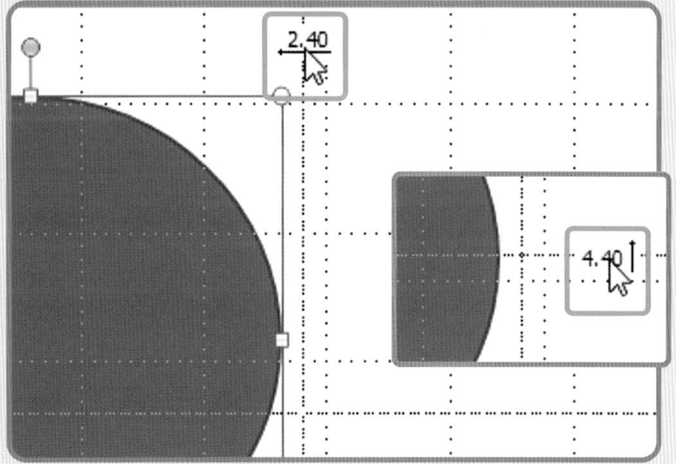

## Key word

***The** Clipboard **is used as a temporary repository for text and other objects which you have copied. It is cleared every time the computer is restarted. You can store up to 24 items on the Clipboard. If you copy more items then the oldest item currently stored on the Clipboard is overwritten.***

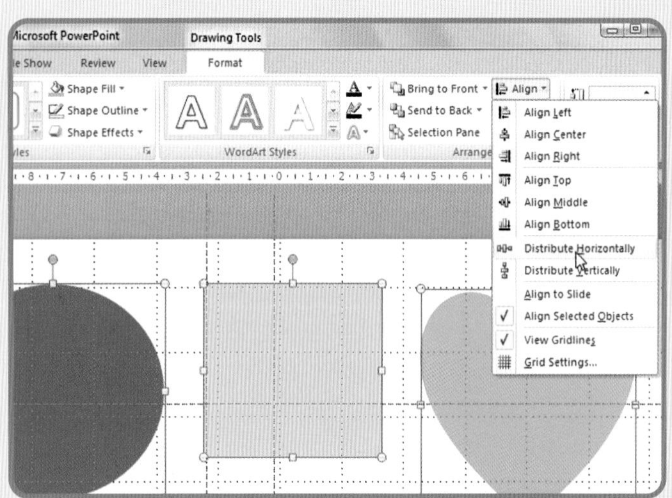


**5** PowerPoint provides several ways to align multiple objects to one another. Hold down the **Shift** key and click each object in turn to select them. Click on the **Format** tab in the Drawing Tools contextual ribbon, then click on **Align** in the Arrange group. Scroll down the list that appears and click on either **Distribute Horizontally** or **Distribute Vertically** to space three or more objects with an equal distance between each one of them. If 'Align to Slide' is selected from the list, the objects will be aligned in relation to the slide itself.

**6** You cannot drag and drop objects between slides. Instead, select the object and cut (**Ctrl** + **X**) or copy (**Ctrl** + **C**) it. This places it on the **Clipboard**. Switch to the slide onto which you want to move the object, click your cursor where you want the object to go and press the keyboard shortcut **Ctrl** + **V** to paste the object onto the slide. You can also copy multiple objects onto the Clipboard, one after another. To paste these, switch to the slide you want them to appear on, click the **Clipboard** dialogue box launcher and then click on an object's thumbnail image in the task pane.

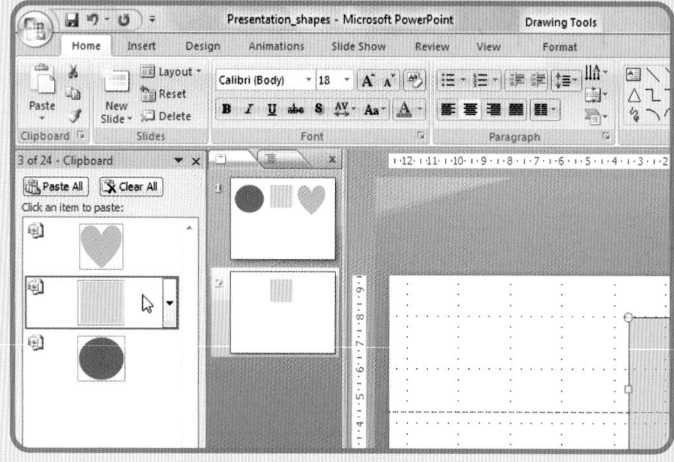

# Automating Tasks

# Using themes

Choosing complementary colours, fonts and special effects for the text, bullet points and background of your presentation is an important ingredient of an eye-catching, professional slide show. PowerPoint has a wide range of pre-defined styles called themes which will help you to get the design right for your presentation.


**SEE ALSO ...**

- *Templates* p26
- *Text boxes & shapes* p44
- *Working with Masters* p56


**BEFORE YOU START**
*First create a new presentation. To do this, click on the **Office** button, then on **New** from the left pane. With **Blank Presentation** highlighted in the middle pane, click on **Create**.*

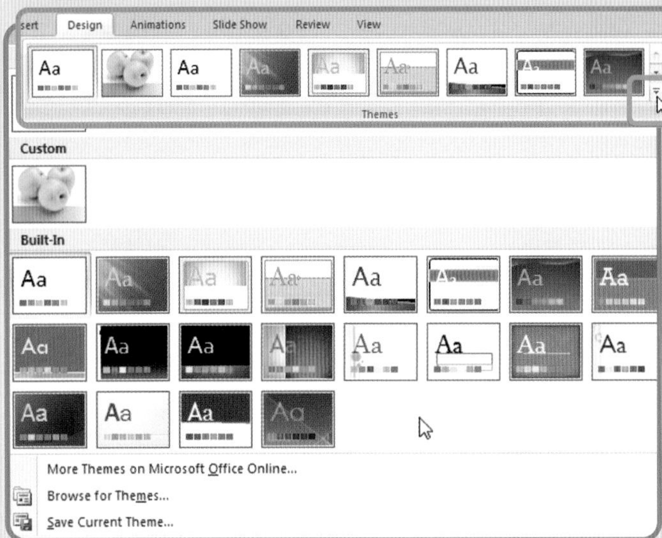


**1** Click on the **Design** tab and choose a theme from the Themes group. A theme is a style for your presentation that includes colours and fonts. If you cannot see a suitable theme, click on the **More** button at the bottom right of the group. There are more themes available here, split into groups: 'This Presentation', which is the current option; 'Custom', which have come from Microsoft Office Online; and 'Built-In', which have been supplied with PowerPoint.

**2** As you move your mouse pointer over the themes within the different groups, your current slide is updated to show how it will look if you decide on a particular theme. A screen tip displays the name of the theme as you do this. It is important to pick a theme that suits the contents of your presentation.

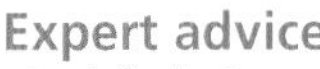

### Expert advice

By default, PowerPoint applies the same theme to every slide of a presentation to avoid confusing the audience by constantly switching between different designs. But if necessary, you can make one slide stand out by using a different theme or different colours. To do this, select the **Design** tab and click on the slide in question. Then right-click on the name of the new theme you have chosen in the Themes group, and choose **Apply to Selected Slides**. Use the same technique to apply a different colour theme to a slide in your presentation.

### Bright idea

***If you can't find a suitable theme from the available selection, and you have an Internet connection, you'll find more themes on the Microsoft Office Web site. To access these click*** *More Themes on Microsoft Office Online* ***from the bottom of the drop-down menu under 'Themes'.***

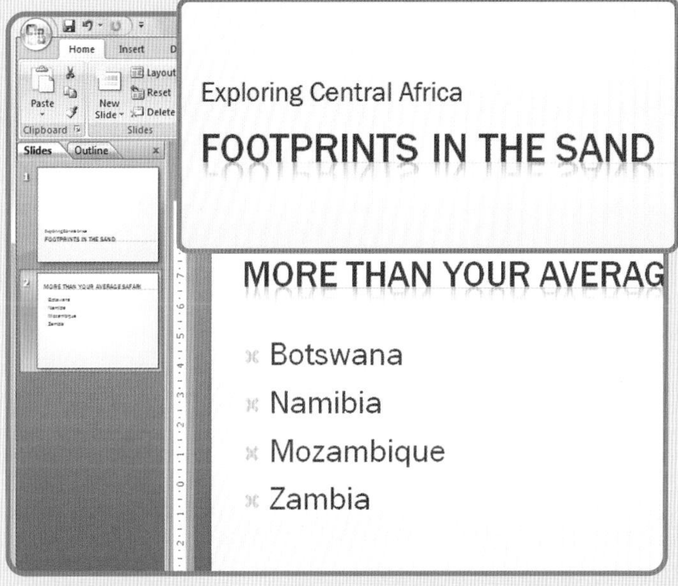


**3** A sandy theme like 'Trek' is perfect for a presentation of a holiday in Africa, for example. Click on a theme to select it. PowerPoint automatically applies that theme to all the slides in your presentation, changing fonts and colours, adding drop-shadows and images to match the theme. Once you have chosen a theme, you can alter various elements such as the colour.

**4** To pick new colours, click on the **Design** tab, if it's not already selected, and then on **Colors** in the Themes group. In the drop-down menu, the colour scheme used by the 'Trek' theme is already selected. As you move your cursor down and over the various 'Built-In' theme colours, your slides update to reflect the new colours incorporated within each theme.

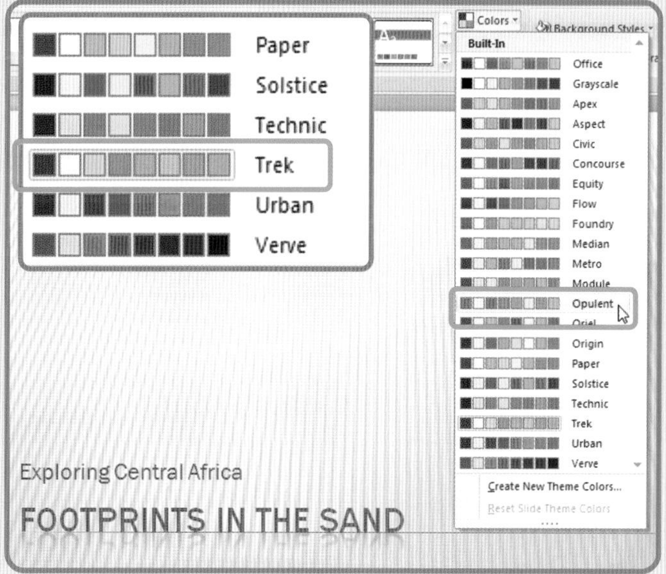

## Adding your own theme colours to the default list

Saving the colour palette you have created as a standard theme colour allows you to use it in any presentation. Once you have chosen colours for the different elements and given the colour palette a name (see Step 6, below), the new theme colour is added to the list of available colours under 'Custom'. To remove it, click on **Colors** in the Themes group and then right-click on the theme name and choose **Delete** from the drop-down menu.

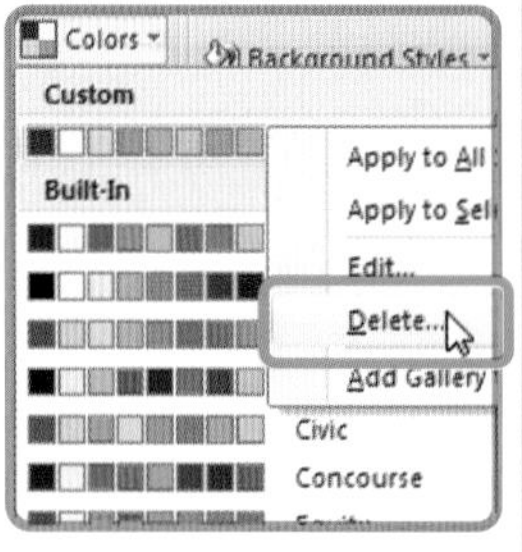

### Expert advice

To quickly change the colour of some text on a single slide, select the text and, with the Home tab selected, click on the arrow next to the Font Color button in the Font group. Choose a new colour from the drop-down menu.

**5** To create new colours, click on **Create New Theme Colors**. In the left pane of the dialogue box you will find a list of colours for your chosen theme, here 'Trek', and a preview under 'Sample' to the right. To change the colour of the title text, for example, click on the arrow next to 'Text/Background - Dark 1', and select from the drop-down menu. The sample on the right updates to reflect your changes. To revert to the original theme colours click on **Reset**.

**6** To select a colour not included in your chosen theme, click on **More Colors**. In the Colors dialogue box choose a new colour from the palette. Click on the **Custom** tab and use the options displayed to fine-tune your choice. When you've finished, click **OK** to confirm. The new colour is displayed under 'Sample' in the right pane. Give your new theme colour a name and click **Save**, or click **Reset** to discard the new colour.

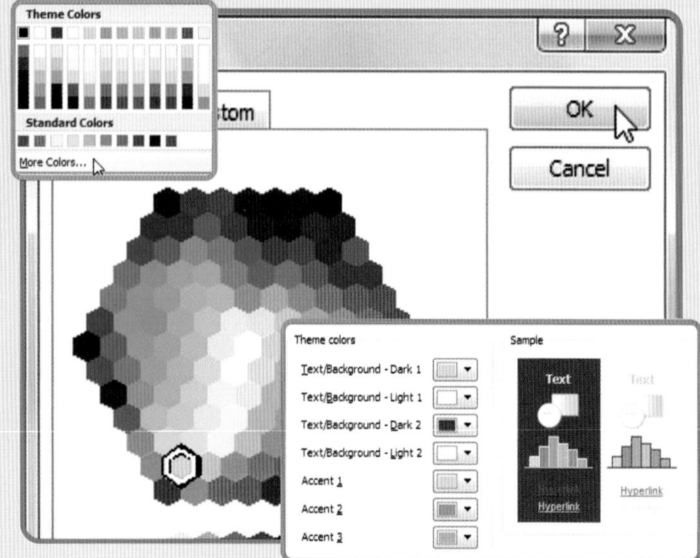

### That's amazing!

PowerPoint offers a selection of different backgrounds using textures, Clip Art and pictures to liven up your presentation. To use these, select the **Design** tab, and click on the **Background** dialogue box launcher. In the Format Background dialogue box make your selection to create an eye-catching background. Click on **Apply to All** to finish.

### Bright idea

***To change the style of a bullet point at the beginning of a line of text, select and right-click on the text and then choose** Bullets. **Select from the drop-down menu of bullet styles that appears or click on the** Bullets and Numbering **option at the bottom of the list.***

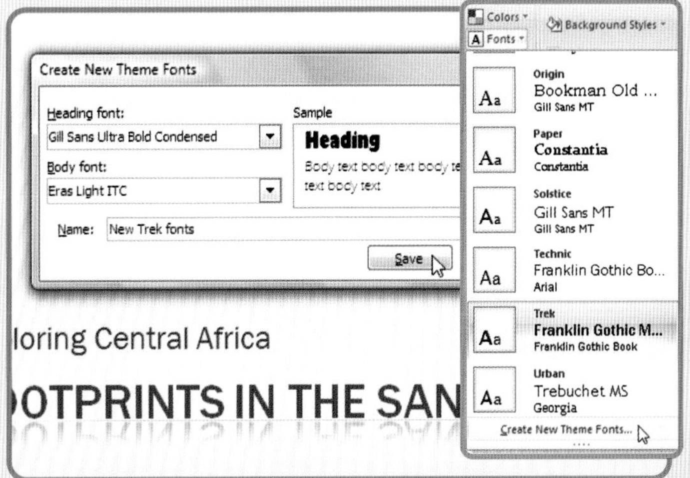


**7** Click on **Fonts** in the Themes group to display a menu of theme names and the fonts attributed to that theme. Each theme font contains a heading and a main text font. You can select a different set of fonts from the list or create your own theme fonts, which can be the same font or complementary ones. Click on **Create New Theme Fonts**, then in the Create New Theme Fonts dialogue box, select fonts from the drop-down menus under 'Heading font' and 'Body font'. Give your theme fonts a name and click on **Save**.

**8** Linked to each theme are theme effects, which are a collection of lines and fills. Unlike colours and fonts you cannot create new or customise existing effects. But you can select a different set of effects from the list to use with your theme. To change the effect linked to your theme, click on **Effects** in the Themes group to display a drop-down menu of effects. Scroll through the list and click to select the effect you think most complements your presentation theme.

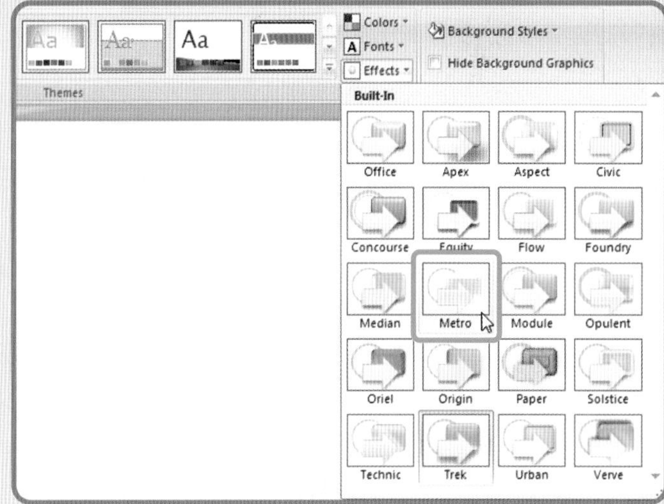

# Working with Masters

Sometimes you may want to include a particular element – such as a logo – on every slide of your presentation. Rather than inserting it on each slide individually, you can place it on a Slide Master, which will make it appear automatically on each one. If you save the Master as a design template, you can use it as the basis for future presentations.

**SEE ALSO ...**


- *Text boxes & shapes* p44
- *Using themes* p52
- *Creating templates* p60


**BEFORE YOU START**

*Open PowerPoint, click on the **Office** button and open a new blank presentation. Click on the **View** tab, then click on **Slide Master** in the Presentation Views group.*

**1** When PowerPoint is in Slide Master view a blank Slide Master with its associated layouts is shown in the slide thumbnail pane on the left. The Slide Master is the larger image found at the top of the pane, with the related layouts below.

**2** You can resize a text box in the Slide Master, in this case to fit a Clip Art image to its left. In the slides pane, click on the text box and drag a square handle to bring the left edge of the box towards the right. To insert the Clip Art image, click on the **Insert** tab, then on **Clip Art** in the Illustrations group.

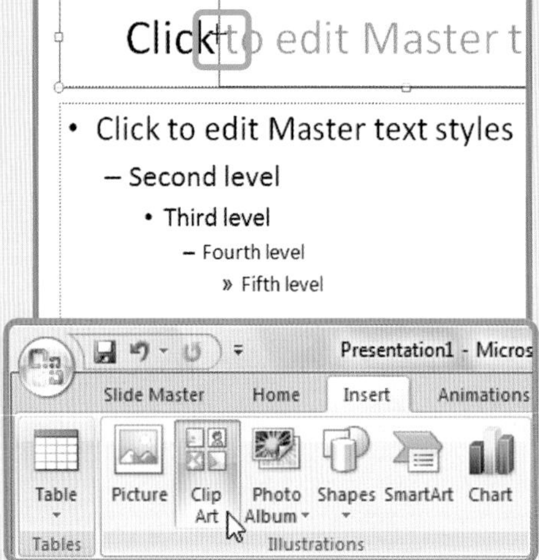

**3** The Clip Art task pane opens. Enter a search term and click on **Go**. Select an image from the search results and click on it to place it on the Master. Move the cursor over a round corner sizing handle and the cursor will change into a double-headed arrow. Click and drag the sizing handles so that the height of the image matches the height of the title text box.

### Expert advice

It isn't just pictures that can be added to a Master – it is possible to add charts (see page 64), additional text fields and any other elements you like. You could, for example, use an extra text field to include your name on every slide of your presentation.

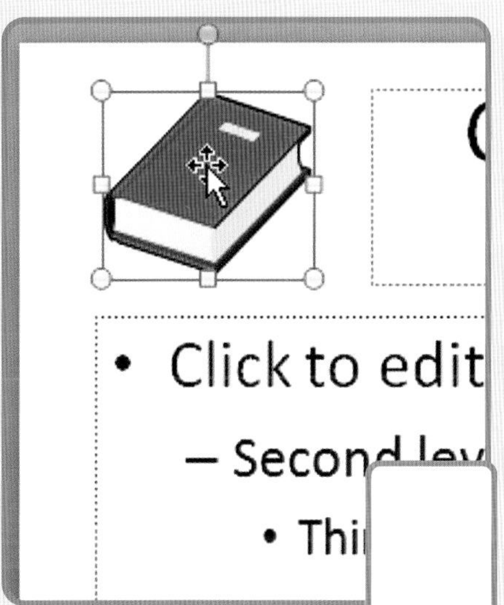


**4** Then move the mouse over the Clip Art graphic so that the cursor turns into a four-headed arrow. Click and drag the graphic to the left of the title text box. Then select **Close Master View** in the Close group, at the far right of the Ribbon. Now, whenever you create a new slide, the logo is inserted automatically.

**5** If you find that none of the default layouts suits your needs, you can create your own layout. Select the **View** tab and click on **Slide Master** in the Presentation Views group, then scroll down the slide thumbnail pane on the left and click below the last layout. Click on the **Slide Master** tab on the Ribbon and then on **Insert Layout** in the Edit Master group.

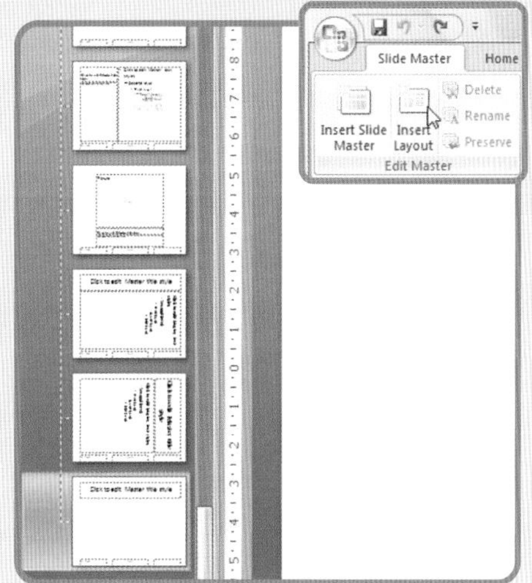

**6** The Title Master slide is now displayed. To remove the default placeholder, click on the border of the placeholder and press **Delete** on the keyboard. To modify and move the various items on the Title Master click on the placeholder border and drag the items to a new position. When you are happy with the design, click on **Close Master View** in the Close group. The master now appears in Normal view and you can start adding your text.

**Bright idea**

***If you have deleted a placeholder and later decide that you need to reinstate it, click the*** *Master Layout* ***button in the Master Layout group and tick the name of the placeholder you want to restore in the dialogue box that appears. Click*** *OK* ***and PowerPoint will add it to the Master again.***

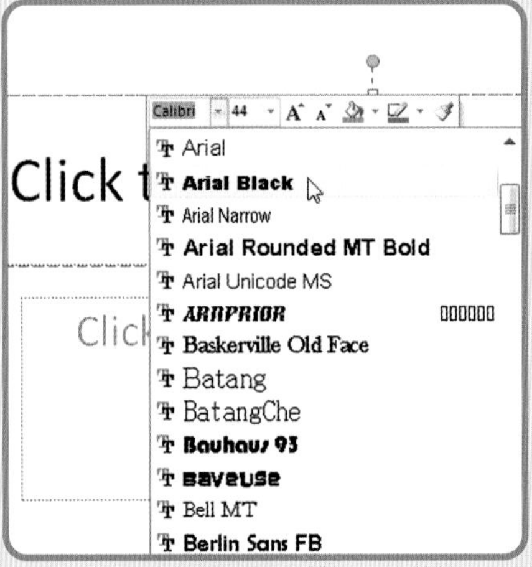


**7** You can also use the Slide Master View to set the fonts used in the various text boxes, and even for different elements within text boxes – the different levels of a list, for example. Right-click on one of the text boxes or elements and then click on the arrow next to the Font box in the Context menu. You can also select the font size, font style and colour of your choice from the Context menu.

**8** To add your own placeholders, click on the **Slide Master** tab and then on **Insert Placeholder** in the Master Layout group. Select the type of placeholder you want to add (here, 'Picture') from the drop-down menu. Then click and drag with the mouse on your layout to position a placeholder where it is needed.

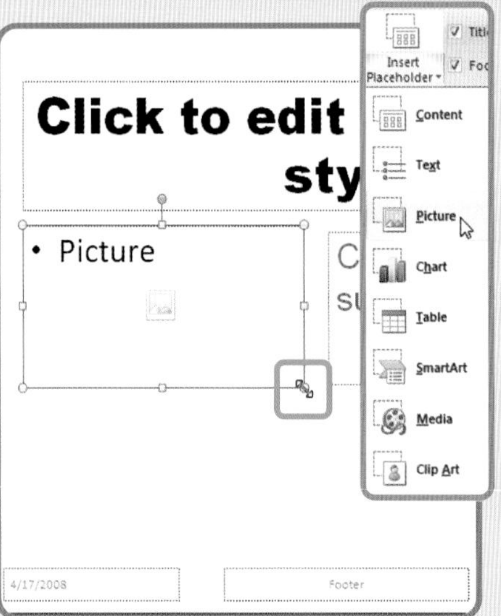


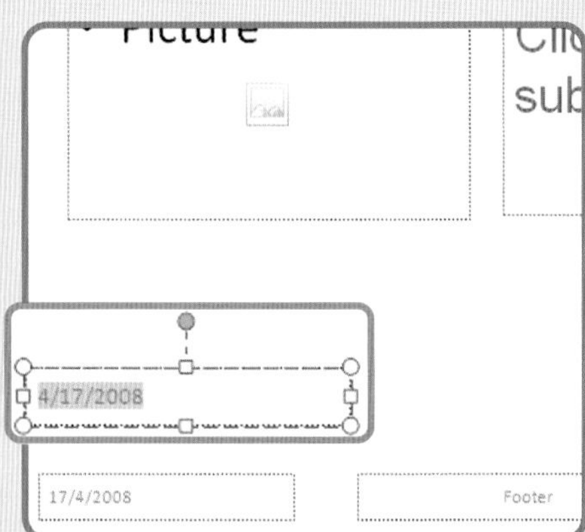


**9** Look for the 'Date' placeholder at the bottom left of the Slide Master. The current date is displayed – but it is probably in the US format (ie month/day/year). To change it to the UK format, double-click with the mouse to select it, then key in the date in the correct format. This could be either the current date or the date on which the presentation is to be made. The text you entered will now appear on every slide except the title slide. The 'Date' placeholder is hidden.

### Expert advice

Once you have created and saved your new customised layout, you can add it to your presentation. Click on the **View** tab and select Normal view, then click on **Layout** in the Slides group. In the drop-down menu your new layout will appear at the bottom of the list. If you haven't renamed it, it will be entitled '1_Custom Layout'.

**10** To apply a uniform background to the title and subsequent slides of your presentation, click on the **Slide Master** tab and, with the Master slide selected, click on any part of the slide outside of the text and picture boxes. Click on **Background Styles** in the Background group and select from the styles in the gallery that appears.

**11** Once you have chosen a style, you can further enhance your background by customising the colour. Click on **Format Background** in the Background styles pane. In the Format Background dialogue box that opens experiment with the fill type, gradient and other options until you are satisfied with the effect. Click on **Apply to All**.

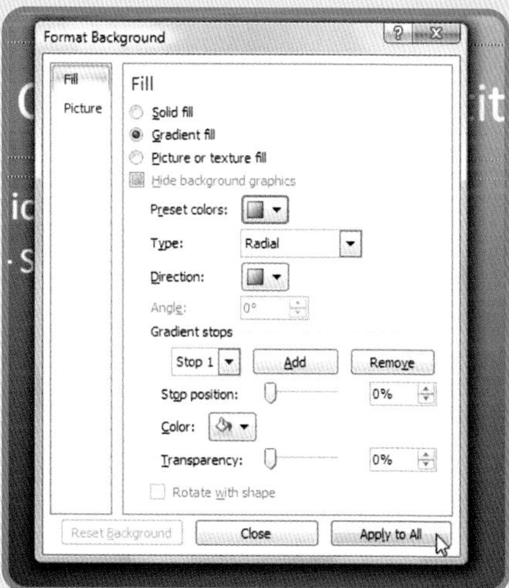


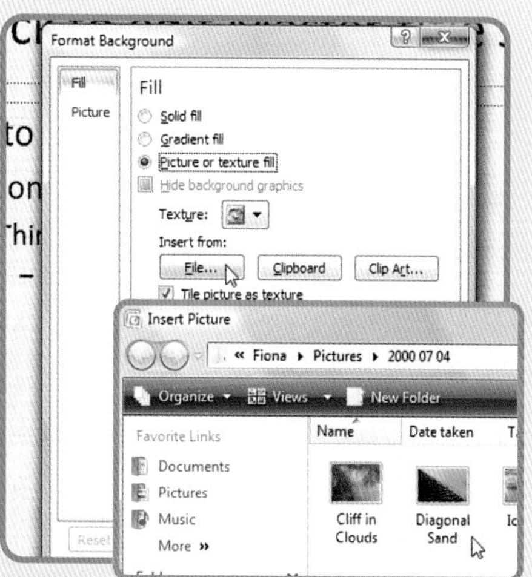


**12** You can use a photo or image as a background. Click on **Format Background** in the Background Styles pane, then click on the radio button next to 'Picture or texture fill' to select it. To choose an image file, click the **File** button under 'Insert from', and in the Insert Picture dialogue box click on an image, then on **Open**. Click on **Apply to All** to add the image to all slides in the presentation.

# Creating your own templates

If you've designed a presentation that you feel is particularly successful, it makes sense to reuse the same style, colour scheme and design in future projects. PowerPoint makes this an easy task – by saving your presentation as a design template you can take all of the elements that you like and repurpose them with different content.


**SEE ALSO ...**

- *Using themes* p52
- *Working with Masters* p56


## WORKING IN SLIDE MASTER VIEW

**To reuse a presentation's font formatting, colours and graphics in a new document without having to use the original content, the settings must be saved in the original file's Slide and Title Masters. To get started, open your finished presentation and switch to Slide Master view by clicking on the** View **tab, then on** Slide Master **in the Presentation Views group (see page 56).**

### Naming the template

Select the **Slide Master** tab and then click on the Master Slide in the left pane. Click on **Rename** in the Edit Master group. In the Rename Master dialogue box, enter a name for the new design template and then click the **Rename** button to confirm the name. Now click on **Preserve** in the Edit Master group. This ensures that the presentation's layout is preserved even when all the slides are deleted. Click **Close Master View** to return to Normal view.

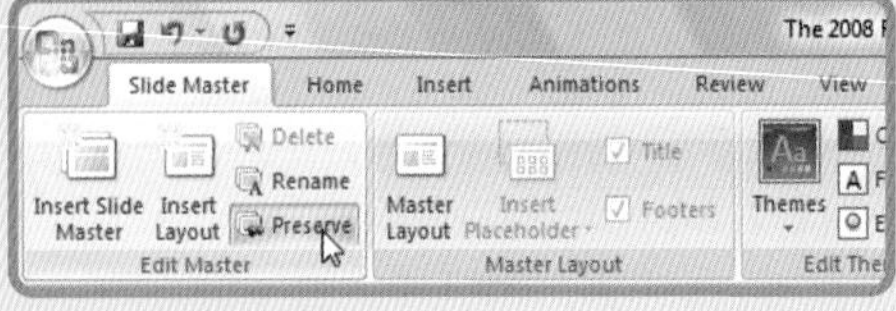


### Deleting slides

In order to delete the slides in your presentation, click on the first slide under the Outline tab on the left-hand side of the screen and scroll down to the bottom. To select all the slides, hold down the **Shift** key as you click the last slide in the presentation. Press the **Delete** key and in the dialogue box that appears click **Yes**. The main PowerPoint workspace is now empty, except for the 'Click to add first slide' text. When you click on the workspace a new slide will appear based on your template. Press **Delete** to remove it.

Click to add first slide

### Saving as a design template

To save the design template for future use, click on the **Office Button** and choose **Save As**. In the Save As dialogue box, click on the arrow next to the 'Save as type' box and choose **PowerPoint Template** from the drop-down menu. In the 'File name' box, enter the same name you used when you renamed the Master. By default, PowerPoint saves the template in the 'Templates' folder, but it may be more useful to save it with the program's other presentation designs. Navigate to your presentations folder and click on **Save**.

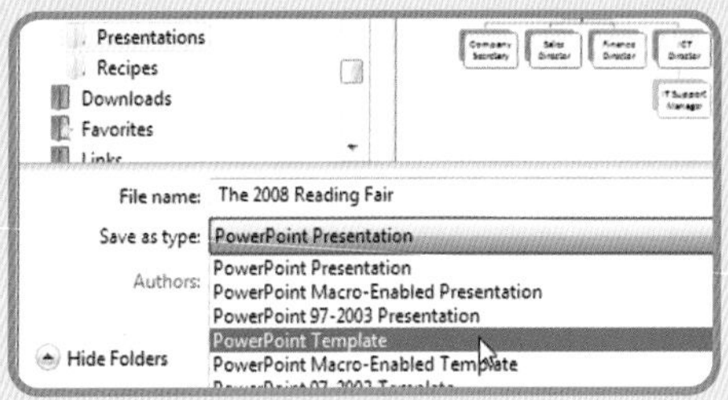


### Using the design template

Start a new presentation by clicking on the **Office Button** and then on **New**. Under 'Templates' in the left panel click on **New from existing** then, in the New from Existing Presentation dialogue box, choose a template, click to select it, then click on **Create New**. A new presentation is created based on the template selected.

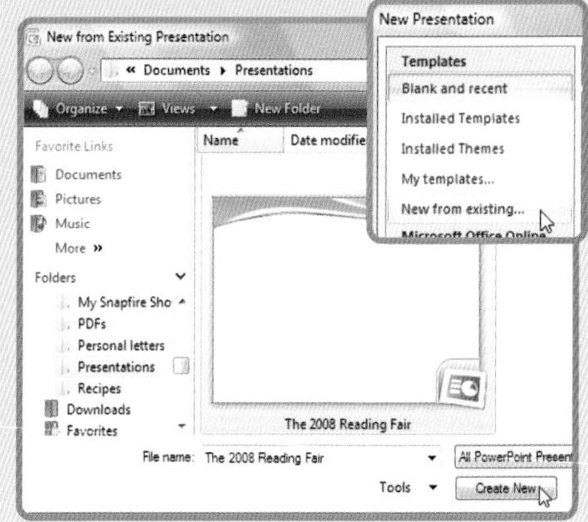

# Embedding Objects

# Creating tables

A table can be one of the best way of presenting facts and figures clearly. In PowerPoint, you can create a table to your specific requirements. And if you realise that your table needs to hold more information than you originally thought, you can add new rows and columns at any point. Deleting unwanted rows and columns is just as simple.

**SEE ALSO ...**

- *Formatting text* p32
- *Arranging objects* p48
- *Inserting charts* p64

**BEFORE YOUR START**

*Tables can be created in various ways, but in all cases you first need to create a presentation. Click on the **Office** button, then on **New**. Select a template and then click on **Create**.*

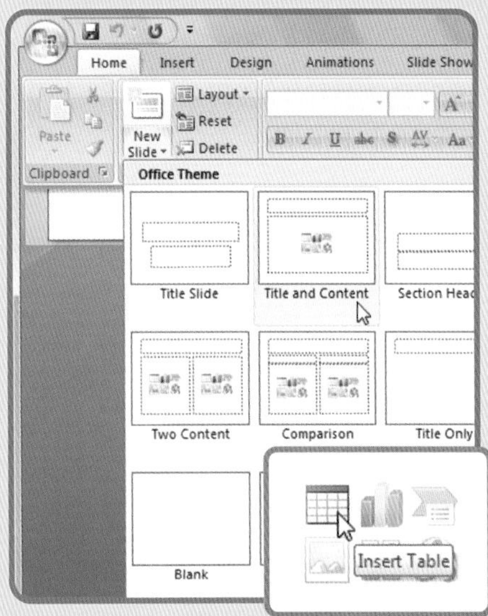


**1** An easy way to create a table is to use a placeholder. Click on the **Home** tab and then in the Slides group, click on the arrow at the bottom of the New Slide button. Select a slide styles that contains a placeholder, here 'Title and Content'. Click on the **Insert Table** icon in the placeholder.

**2** The Insert Table dialogue box will open. Select the number of columns and rows you require and click **OK**. Your table will appear on the slide. To enter data, click in a cell and type. Press the Tab key to go to the next cell, or use the Arrow keys to move in any direction. Format the text as in a normal text box. To select multiple cells, hold down the mouse button and drag the mouse over the cells you require.

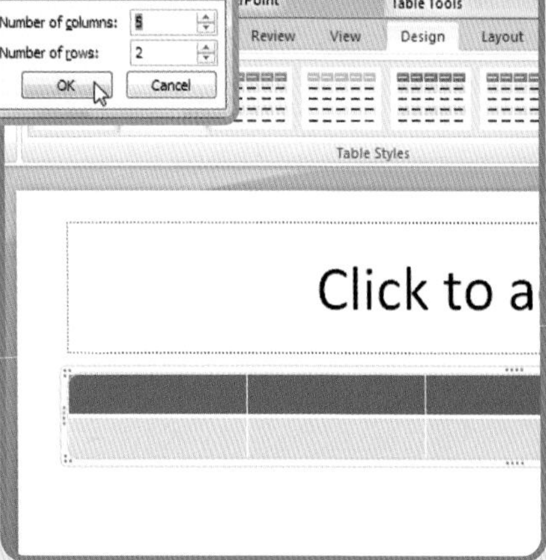


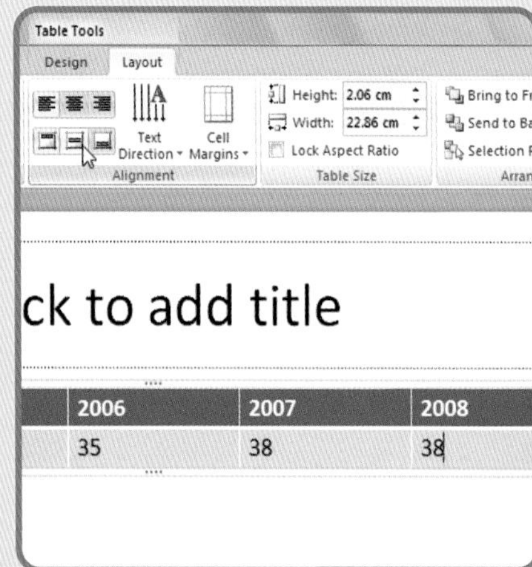


**3** By default, PowerPoint aligns any text vertically along the top edge of the cell and horizontally to the left of the cell. You can align text to the middle or bottom of cells, or change the horizontal alignment to centred or right. First, select one or more cells containing text then click on the **Layout** tab in the Table Tools contextual ribbon and use the Alignment group buttons to realign your text as you want.

### Expert advice

Another way to insert a table is to click on the **Insert** tab and then on **Table** in the Tables group. You can use the grid that appears to select the number of rows and columns required and click the mouse to confirm. Alternatively, select **Insert Table** from the drop-down menu under the grid and you'll be presented with the Insert Table dialogue box described in Step 2.

### Merging and splitting cells

You can merge neighbouring cells both vertically and horizontally to create a single cell. Select the cells you want to merge, click on the **Layout** tab in the Table Tools contextual ribbon, and then click on **Merge Cells** in the Merge group. Similarly, you can split a cell by clicking on **Split Cells** in the Merge group.

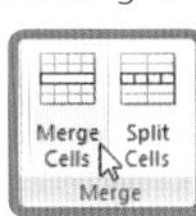


Then, in the Split Cells dialogue box that appears, enter the number of columns and rows you require, and click on **OK**.

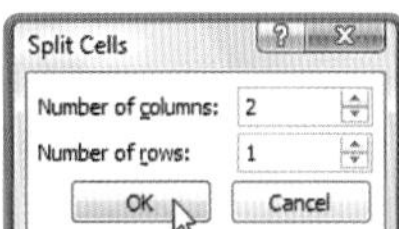


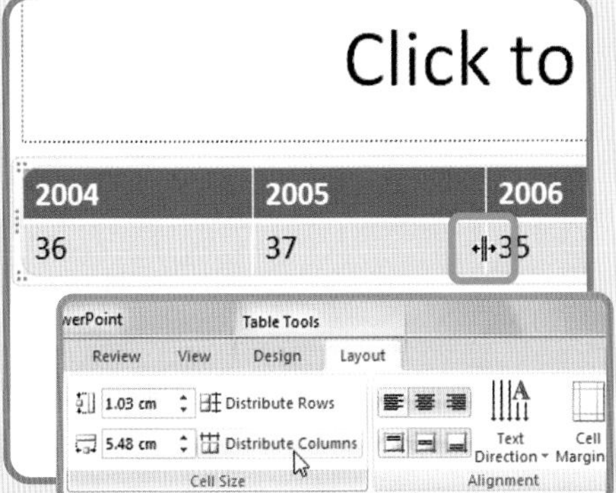


**4** To adjust the width of a column, move the cursor over one of its boundary lines then, when the cursor changes into two parallel lines with an arrow either side, click and drag with the mouse. The columns on either side of the line enlarge or reduce in width accordingly. Release the mouse button when you are satisfied. To make specific columns an equal width, select them, then click on the **Layout** tab in the Table Tools contextual ribbon and click on **Distribute Columns** in the Cell Size group.

**5** You can change the number of rows and columns at any time. To add a new row beneath an existing one, for example, place the cursor within the existing row, and click on the **Layout** tab in the Table Tools contextual ribbon, then click on **Insert Below** in the Rows & Columns group. Use the same procedure to insert columns. To delete rows or columns and their contents, click on **Delete**, then on **Delete Columns** or **Delete Rows** from the drop-down menu.

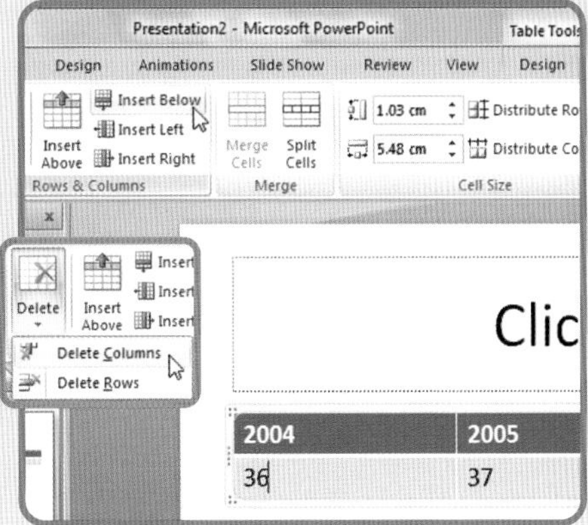


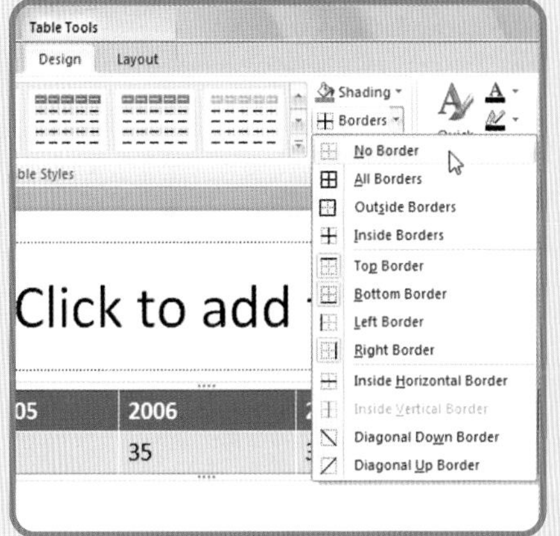


**6** To change the look of the cell boundary lines, select the cells of the borders you want to adjust. Click on the **Design** tab and in the Table Styles group click on the arrow next to the Borders button and select from the drop-down menu. Click on **No Border** to hide the boundary lines. To apply more than one border option, click each one in turn while holding down the **Shift** key. Click on the **Shading** and **Effects** buttons for more formatting options.

# Inserting charts

Figures and statistics are much easier to understand if you present them as charts. The visual clarity that they bring will help your audience to compare different sets of data and identify trends more easily. With PowerPoint's built-in graphing feature you can create and format diagrams to suit the information they contain in no time at all.

**SEE ALSO ...**

- *Pictures & Clip Art* p38

**BEFORE YOU START**

*Insert a new slide by clicking on the arrow next to New Slide in the Slides group and then on the **Title Only** layout (see page 30). Then apply a basic theme (see page 52).*

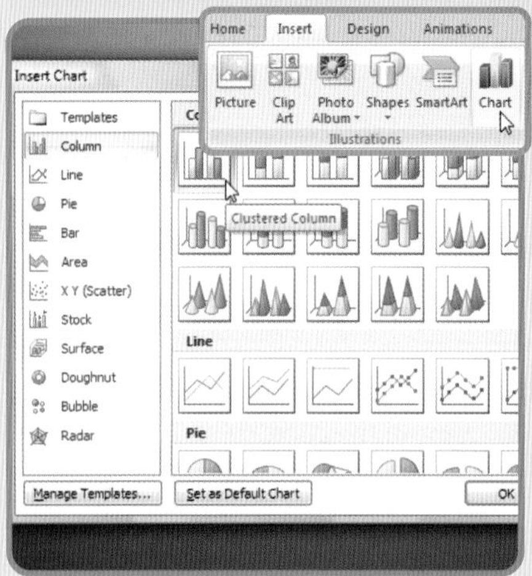


**1** Enter a title for the slide. Then click on the **Insert** tab and then on **Chart** in the Illustrations group. In the Insert Chart dialogue box that appears, select a chart type from the left pane and then click on a chart sub-type in the right pane.

Alternatively, you can use the default chart type supplied, which is called 'Clustered Column'. In both cases click on **OK** to close the dialogue box.

**2** PowerPoint inserts a chart with dummy data on the slide and shows the data in a Microsoft Excel spreadsheet in a separate window. Put your figures and headings into the spreadsheet. To add a column or row, enter data into the cells and click and drag the lower right-hand corner of the range boundary to include the data in the chart. To delete a column or row, right-click on the column heading or row number and choose **Delete**.

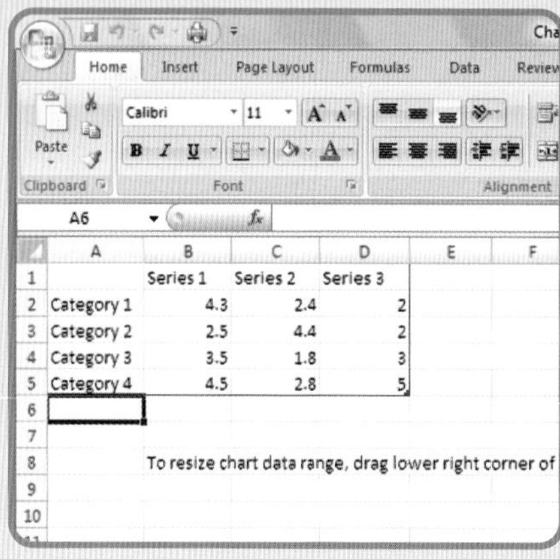


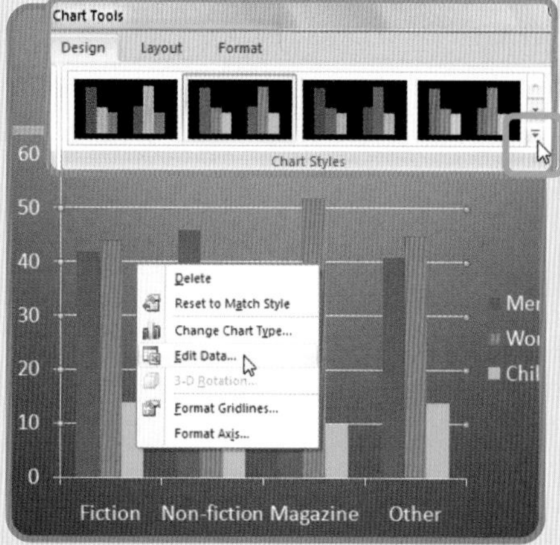


**3** Close the Excel window and your slide will display the bar chart PowerPoint has created. To edit the chart you will need to go back into the Excel spreadsheet. To do this, right-click inside the chart and click on **Edit Data** from the drop-down menu. To change the colour scheme, double-click on the chart and then click on a style in the Chart Styles group. For more style options, click on the arrow at the bottom right of the Chart Styles group.

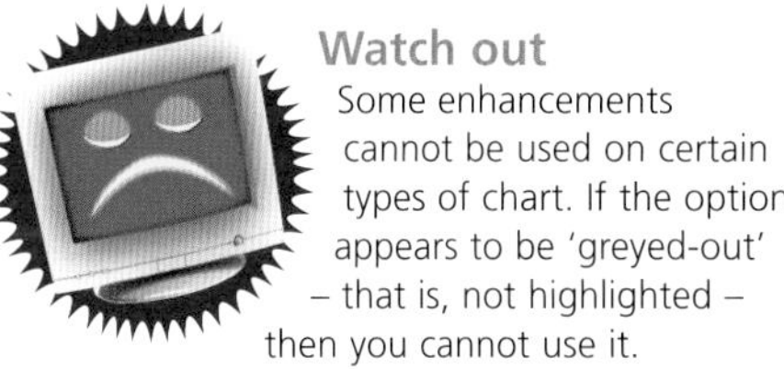

### Watch out

Some enhancements cannot be used on certain types of chart. If the option appears to be 'greyed-out' – that is, not highlighted – then you cannot use it.

### Expert advice

If right-clicking on an element of a chart does not reveal an option to edit that element, then the chart itself is probably not selected. Double-click on the chart so that it is surrounded by a dashed line with eight sizing handles. You will then be able to access the chart commands.

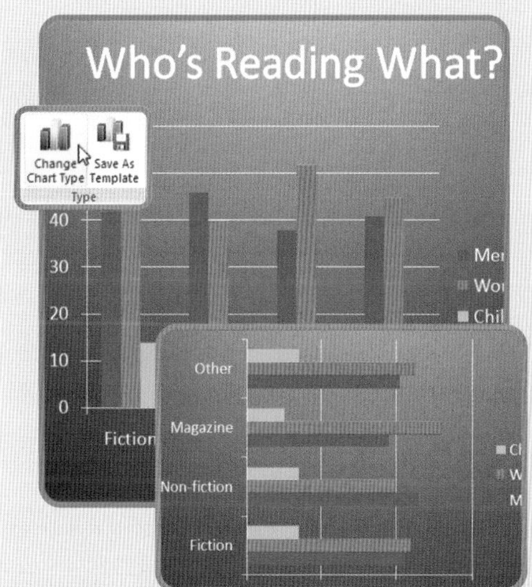


**4** To change to another type of chart, double-click on the chart you want to alter and then click on **Change Chart Type** in the Type group. In the Change Chart Type dialogue box, select a basic chart type from the left pane, 'Bar' for example, and then click on a chart sub-type in the right pane. Click on **OK** to finish.

**5** Once you are happy with the look of the chart, you can add enhancements to make the chart more meaningful and as clear as possible. Click on the **Layout** tab in the Chart Tools contextual ribbon and then on **Data Labels** in the Labels group. Select a style from the drop-down menu, here 'Outside End'. This displays the exact value at the end of each data point within the chart.

| | Fiction | Non-fiction | Magazine | Other |
|---|---|---|---|---|
| Children | 14 | 14 | 10 | 14 |
| Women | 44 | 40 | 52 | 45 |
| Men | 42 | 46 | 38 | 41 |

**6** You can add as much embellishment as you like to the graph. You can choose to display or hide both axes and gridlines, or you can change the format of individual elements within your chart.

You can also display the data below the chart. Select the **Layout** tab, click on **Data Table** in the Labels group and then click on **Show Data Table**.

To undo any changes you have made click on **Reset to Match Style** in the Current Selection group.

# Music & sounds

Background music and sound effects, if used in a sympathetic way, can really enhance a presentation. They help to attract and keep the audience's attention – particularly useful if the presentation has been set up to run automatically. In PowerPoint, you can insert any music or sound file you like into your presentation. You can also play music from an audio CD.

**SEE ALSO ...**

- *Slide shows* p92
- *Recording a narration* p96

**BEFORE YOU START**

*Create a new presentation containing multiple slides or open an existing one. Make a copy of the presentation so that you still have the original if you want a version without sound.*

**1** Click on the **Insert** tab on the Ribbon and then on the arrow on the Sound button in the Media Clips group. Click on **Sound from File** and in the Insert Sound dialogue box navigate to the 'Sample Music' folder. Here you will find a selection of tracks from Rock to Classical. Click on the file you want and then on **Open**.

**2** PowerPoint asks whether the sound should play automatically whenever the slide is opened, or only when the sound file icon is clicked on. Click on **Automatically** and a loudspeaker icon appears in the middle of the slide. Make sure that the icon is selected, then use the mouse to click and drag it to a suitable place on the slide. When you next present the slide, the music will start automatically. Click on the loudspeaker icon to start the music again or move to the next slide to stop the music.

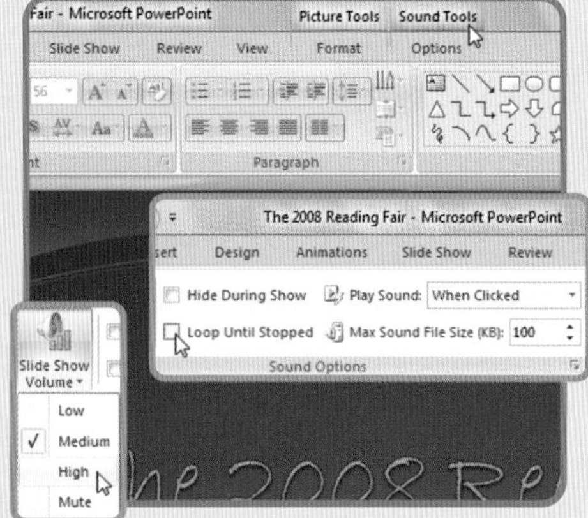

**3** If the music finishes before you are ready to move to the next slide, you can set it to loop so that it repeats continuously. To activate this, click on the loudspeaker icon on the slide, then on the **Sound Tools** contextual tab that appears on the Title bar. In the Sound Options group, add a tick next to 'Loop Until Stopped'. You can set the volume by clicking on the arrow on the Slide Show Volume button, in the same group, and selecting from the drop-down menu.

### Bright idea

***If you have set music to play automatically, the loudspeaker symbol isn't usually required and can therefore be hidden. Click on the icon, then on the** Options **tab in the Sound Tools contextual ribbon. Then tick** Hide During Show **in the Sound Options group.***

### Watch out

If your presentation includes sound files and you want to ensure that it can be played on other PCs without any problems, you should make sure that the sound files are saved with a .wav file extension and that the sound file is under 100KB in size. PowerPoint will then embed the files in the presentation. All other file types are linked rather than embedded in the presentation. This means that they must be in exactly the same folders on your computer when you play the presentation as they were when you created it.

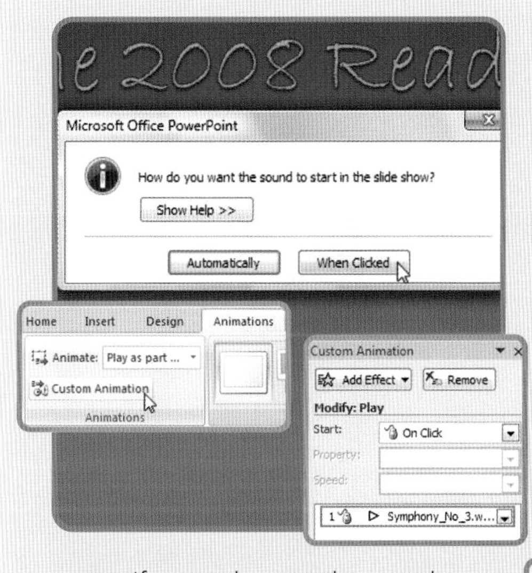


**4** If you only want the sound to play when the loudspeaker icon is clicked on, choose **When Clicked** at the prompt in Step 2. Move the loudspeaker icon to a suitable position on the slide. Click on the **Animations** tab and then on **Custom Animation** in the Animations group. The Custom Animation task pane will appear on the right of the window.

**5** To ensure that the music continues until you move to the next slide in the presentation, click on the arrow next to the track title in the task pane and then on **Timing**. The Play Sound dialogue box will open. From the drop-down menu next to 'Repeat', select 'Until End of Slide'. You can control the volume under the Sound Settings tab of the same dialogue box. Click on **OK** to confirm.

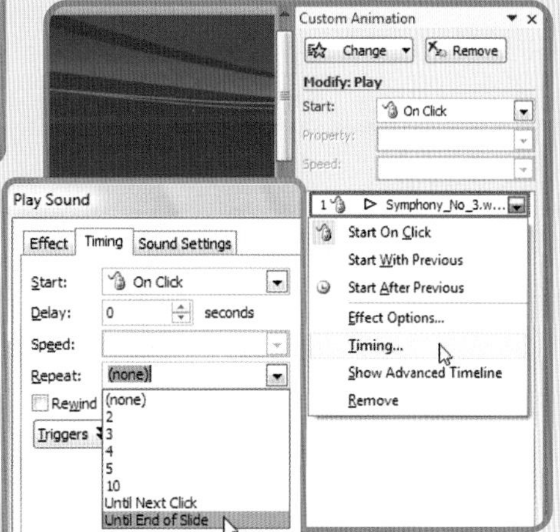


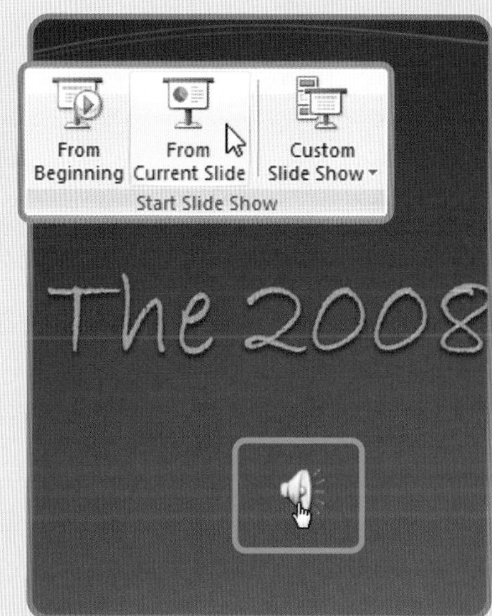


**6** To start the slide show, click the **Slide Show** tab on the Ribbon and choose **From Current Slide** in the Start Slide Show group. The music starts when you click on the loudspeaker icon and ends when you move to the next slide, either automatically or by clicking the mouse.

### That's amazing!

To check the sound on a particular slide without having to play the entire presentation to get to it, right-click your mouse on the loudspeaker icon and in the Context menu select **Preview**.

### Bright idea

***If you encounter any problems when adding sound to your presentation, click on the*** *Help* ***icon found at the far right of the Ribbon. In the PowerPoint Help dialogue box that appears type 'sound' into the Search panel. Scroll down the list of results and select one of the help options. If you are connected to the Internet, you'll now have access to the latest information from Microsoft on your topic.***

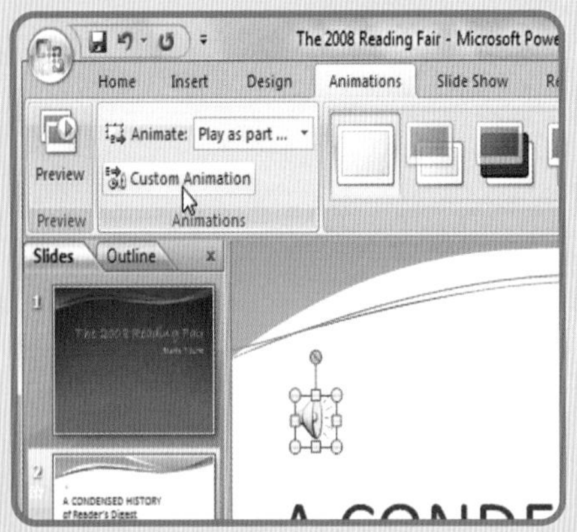


**7** In many presentations, the first and last slides are simply used to greet and bid farewell to the audience. When that is the case, it may be better to start the music on the second slide, and finish it on the penultimate slide. To do this, go to the second slide, insert the music you want, and when asked click **Automatically**. Then, with the loudspeaker icon selected, click on the **Animations** tab on the Ribbon and then on **Custom Animation** in the Animations group.

**8** In the Custom Animation task pane, click on the arrow to the right of your chosen track and then on **Effect Options** in the drop-down menu. Click on the **Effect** tab of the Play Sound dialogue box then in the 'Stop playing' section, select the 'After: ... slides' option and enter the number of slides during which the music should play, including the current slide. Click on **OK** to confirm the settings.

**9** To automatically play music from a CD during a presentation, first put the CD in your CD drive. Click on the **Insert** tab, then on the down arrow under 'Sound' in the Media Clips group. Now click on **Play CD Audio Track** in the drop-down menu. PowerPoint displays the Insert CD Audio dialogue box which shows the number of tracks on the CD you inserted and their total playing time.

### Watch out

If your computer has more than one CD drive, note that PowerPoint will only recognise audio CDs and allow you to use their tracks as sounds when they are inserted in the drive with the lowest drive letter. So if your D: and E: drives are both CD drives, place your CD in the D: drive.

### Expert advice

If you change your mind and want to turn a sound that plays automatically into one that plays only when clicked upon, click on the loudspeaker icon then on the **Animations** tab and choose **Custom Animation**. In the Custom Animation task pane under 'Modify: Play', select **Start on click** from the 'Start' drop-down menu. Similarly, to turn a sound that starts only when clicked into one that starts automatically, open the Custom Animation task pane and select **After Previous** from the drop-down menu next to 'Start'.

**10** In the 'Clip selection' area of the dialogue box, choose the CD track that you want the presentation soundtrack to start with and the track that you want it to end with. If you only want to play one track from the CD, enter the same track number in both the 'Start at track' and 'End at track' boxes. Then click on **OK**.

**11** It isn't just music that can be used to enhance your presentation. You can also add sound effects – such as the sound of running water. If you don't already have the effect you want held as a sound file or on CD, PowerPoint lets you record it yourself using a microphone. To do so, click on the **Insert** tab, then on the down arrow under the Sound button in the Media Clips group. Now click on **Record Sound** from the drop-down menu. This opens the Record Sound dialogue box.

**12** Make sure you have a microphone attached (see page 96), enter a name for the new sound file and press the button with the red dot on it to start recording. Create the sound and then click the button marked with a blue rectangle to stop the recording. The length of the recorded sound is displayed below the name. Click **OK** to insert the sound into your presentation.

# Using Organization Charts

If you are using PowerPoint to introduce a company or club, the organisation's personnel structure is likely to be an important aspect of your presentation. Organization Charts are a special type of diagram used to represent exactly this kind of structure. PowerPoint's built-in editor lets you add and customise a sample chart to your own requirements in a few easy steps.

**SEE ALSO ...**

- *Pictures & Clip Art* p38
- *Inserting charts* p64

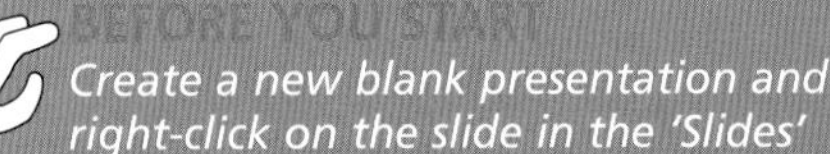

**BEFORE YOU START**

*Create a new blank presentation and right-click on the slide in the 'Slides' pane. Select **Layout** and click on **Title Only**. Click on the title placeholder and enter a heading.*

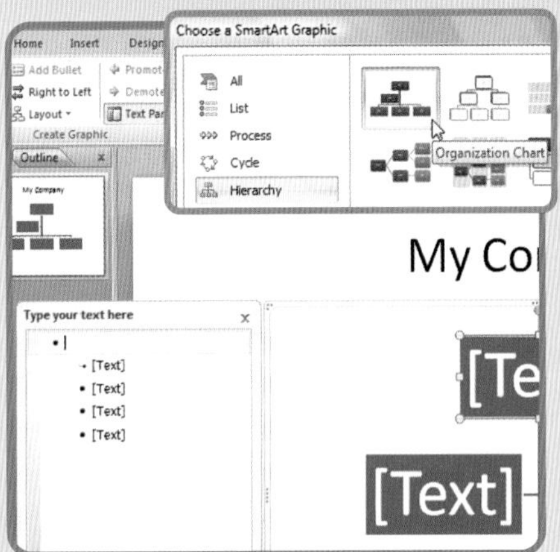


**1** Select the **Insert** tab on the Ribbon, then click on **Smart Art** in the Illustrations group. In the dialogue box that opens click on **Hierarchy** in the left pane then select a style from the middle pane, here 'Organization Chart', and click on **OK**. A sample chart is inserted comprising four boxes, with the box at the top of the hierarchy – for the head – selected. To the left of the chart is the text pane in which to add your text.

**2** Enter the names and/or roles of the people in the organisation into the relevant text boxes in the text pane. If there is more text than will fit in the box, the box size will not change but PowerPoint will automatically adjust the font size of the text and extra lines will be created.

Type your text here
- Managing Director
- Company Secretary
- Sales Director
- Finance Director
- ICT Director

My Company
Managing Director
Company Secretary
Sales Director
Finance Director
ICT Director

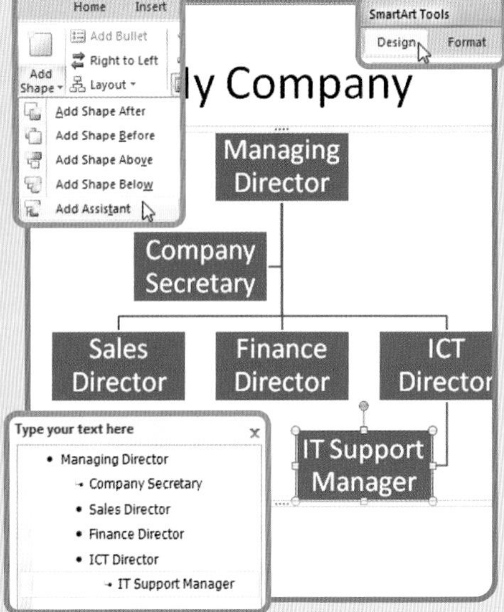


**3** To make the chart larger, click on a box then, with the SmartArt Tools contextual ribbon active, click on the **Design** tab. Now click on **Add Shape** in the Create Graphic group and select **Add Assistant** from the drop-down menu. Enter text for the new box in the text pane.

**Bright idea**

***If you want to use your chart in other programs or presentations, save it as a separate image by right-clicking on the chart and choosing*** *Save As Picture* ***from the drop-down menu. In the Save As Picture dialogue box select a location in which to save the file, type in a file name and in the 'Save as type' box choose a picture format, for example, TIFF (Tag Image File Format), and then click on*** *Save*.

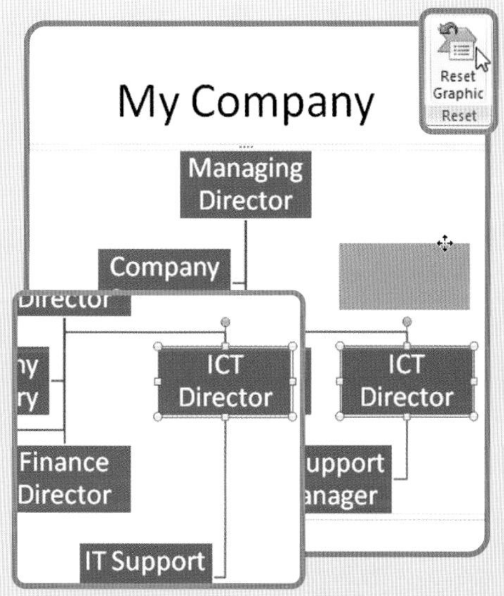


**4** To move individual entries to a new position in the company structure, select the box you want to move by clicking on its border (not on its text) and dragging the shape to its new position. The connecting line or lines are redrawn automatically. If you change your mind, click on **Reset Graphic** in the Reset group.

**5** You don't have to start again if you want to use a different layout for your chart. Click on a box in the chart, then with the SmartArt Tools contextual ribbon active, click on the **Design** tab. Hover your mouse pointer over the icons in the Layouts group, and your chart will automatically adopt the different styles as you do so. Click on the **More** button at the bottom right of the Layout group to see additional layouts. Click on a new layout to select it.

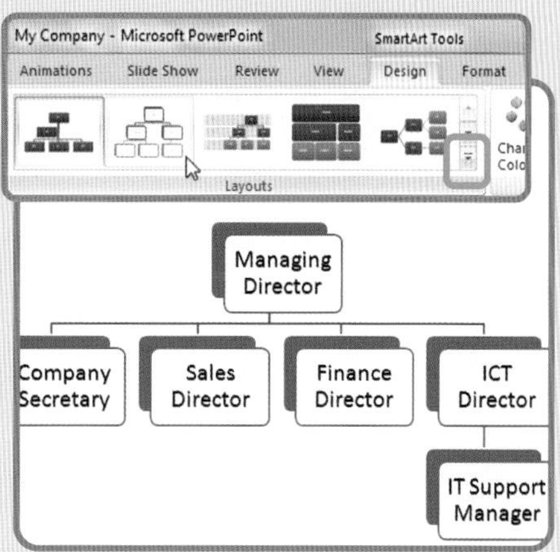


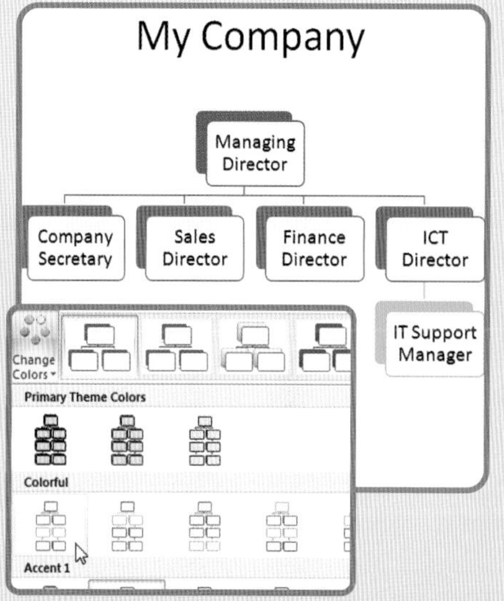


**6** To change the style of your chart, select one of the style options from the SmartArt Styles group under the Design tab in the SmartArt Tools contextual ribbon. To change the colour, click on **Change Colors** in the same group. Hover the cursor over the colour icons to preview the schemes. Click on a colour scheme to select it.

# WordArt

Adding colourful, three-dimensional text is a great way to inject some fun into your presentation. PowerPoint gives you access to Microsoft Office's WordArt feature, where you'll find a variety of decorative text effects. You can make your text more dramatic by giving it a different colour outline, or rotate your words so that they read at an angle.

**SEE ALSO ...**

- *Pictures & Clip Art* p38
- *Using themes* p52

BEFORE YOU START

*Start PowerPoint and either create a new presentation or open an existing one. Add a new slide to the presentation using the* ***Title Only*** *layout (see page 30).*

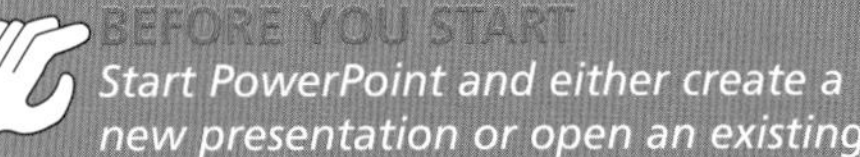


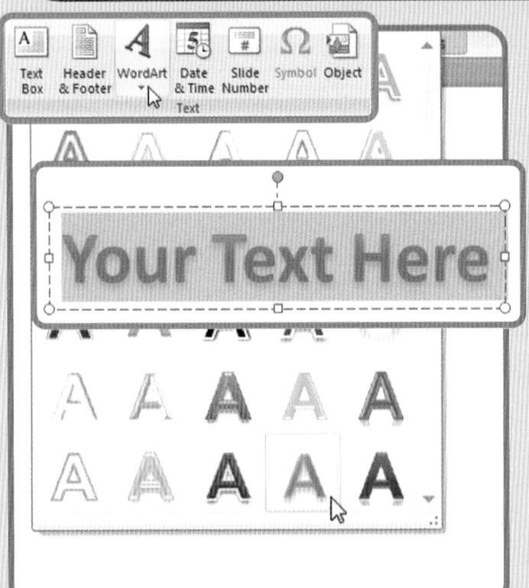


**1** Give your slide a title. Click on the **Insert** tab, then on **WordArt** in the Text group. The WordArt gallery offers a range of slides that you can choose from. When you select one, the default text 'Your Text Here' is displayed in a bounding box – a text box that automatically expands or shrinks to fit your text. Replace the sample text with your own text.

**2** To change the size of the text that you have added, highlight it, then move your mouse and the Mini Toolbar is displayed. Select a new size from the drop-down menu next to the font size box in the Mini Toolbar. Click and drag the green circle handle left or right to rotate the WordArt object along its horizontal axis. The cursor turns into a circle with arrows and a dashed outline indicates the new position.

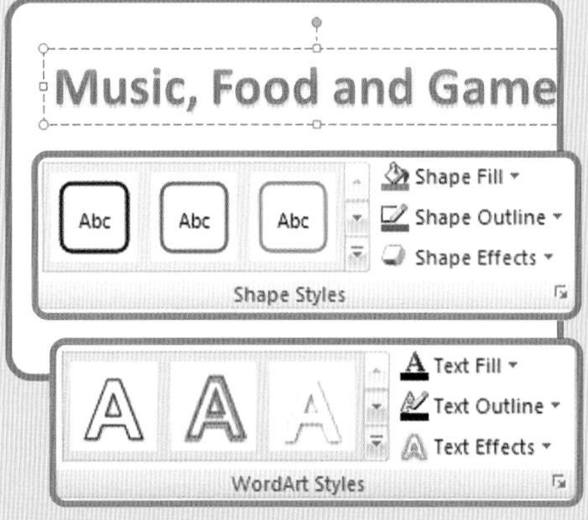


**3** The Drawing Tools contextual ribbon is now displayed. Click on the **Format** tab. In the Shape Styles group, you can change the colours used for 'Shape Fill' and 'Shape Outline' and choose from options in 'Shape Effects'. Additionally, in the WordArt Styles group you can change the 'Text Fill' and 'Text Outline' colours and choose from the 'Text Effects' options. Experiment with these styles, but remember not to include too many different ones as it will look confusing.

# Organising your Presentation

# Structuring presentations

When you create a presentation, you usually enter text on a series of consecutive slides. You will often want to arrange the text within each slide into main points and sub-points, and you may later decide to restructure your presentation and move some points to a different slide. These tasks are best performed using PowerPoint's Outline tab.


**SEE ALSO ...**

- *First steps* p20
- *Using lists* p36
- *Arranging objects* p48


**BEFORE YOU START**
*Create a new presentation comprising four or five slides. The presentation can be on any topic but at least two of the slides should contain lists with several points in each.*

**1** You can see preview images of each slide in the presentation in the pane on the left of the document window. There are two tabs above the images: Slides (indicated by a rectangular symbol if the pane is too narrow to fit the actual word) and Outline (indicated by several lines, rather like a paragraph of right-aligned text). Click on the **Outline** tab.

**2** The Outline tab shows all the text in the presentation, slide by slide. The slide titles appear in bold text and the icon of the current slide is indicated with a blue frame around it. Where slides contain lists, the bullet points are also visible. To switch to another slide, click on the content of the slide you wish to select in the Outline tab. Another way to navigate is to use the scroll bar found on the right of the PowerPoint window to move back and forth between the slides.

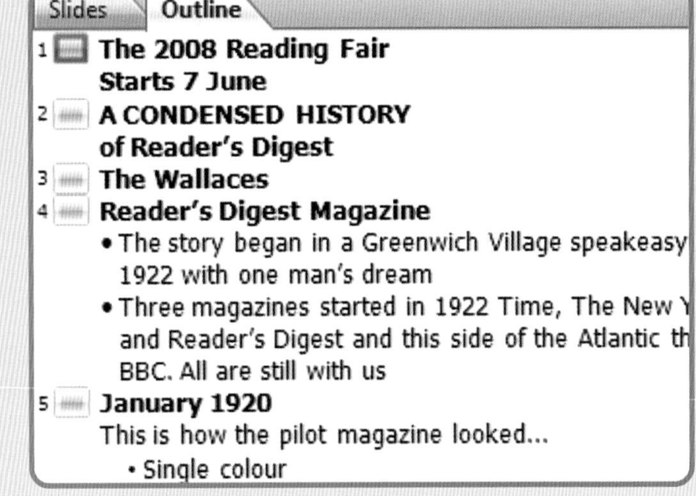

## Bright idea

***If you have accidentally closed the pane containing the Outline tab or you can't see it when you open a presentation, click on the*** *View* ***tab on the Ribbon and then on*** *Normal* ***in the Presentation Views group.***

## Expanding all text

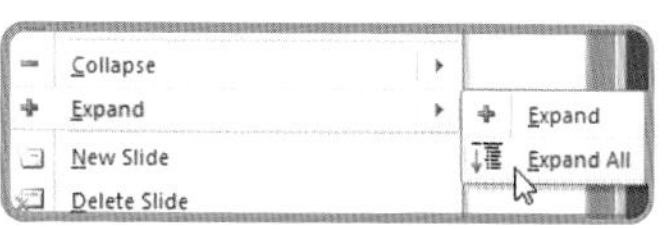


To quickly show or hide all the text beneath all the headings in PowerPoint's Outline tab, simply right-click on a heading and from the drop-down menu click on **Expand**, then **Expand All**.
To collapse all the text to show only the headings, right-click on a slide and then, from the drop-down menu, click on **Collapse**, then **Collapse All**.

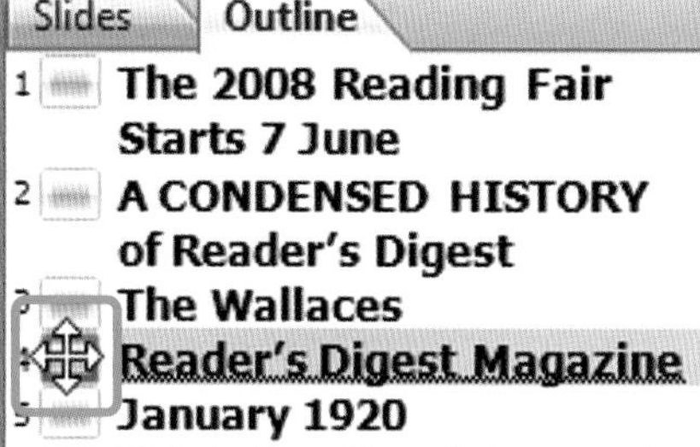


**3** To get a clear overview of your presentation, you can collapse the content of slides so that only their titles are visible in the Outline tab. To do this, move the mouse point to the left side of the Outline tab. The mouse pointer turns into a white four-headed arrow. Double-click on one of the slide icons. A grey line appears under the title to indicate that the text is hidden. Repeat this process for every slide.

Note that this change does not affect the slides, where the text remains visible. Double-click on the slide icons to reveal the hidden text.

**4** The Outline tab is ideal if you want to move individual sections of text around. First, select the section that you want to move. Move the mouse pointer to the beginning of the section you want to select and it will turn into a four-headed arrow again. Then click once to select the entire section. To select several sections of text in one go, hold down the **Shift** key as you click at the beginning of each section in turn.

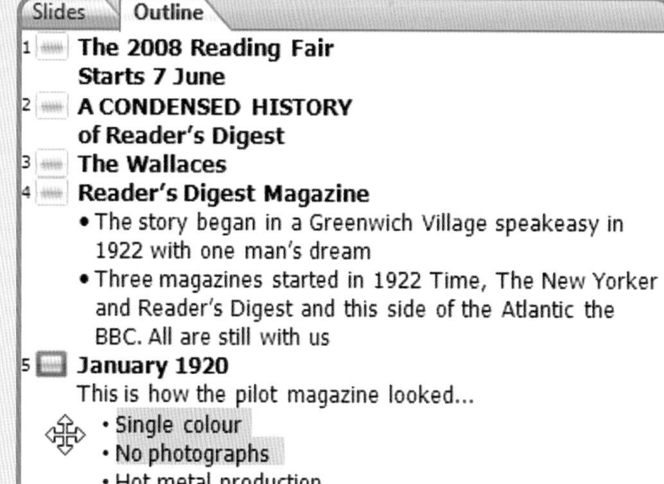

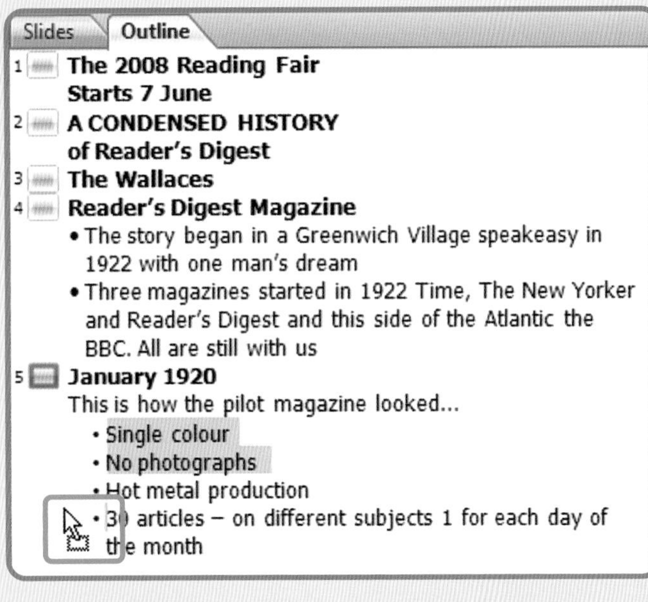


**5** To move the text, click on your selection and hold down the mouse button as you drag the text to its new position. A small rectangle with a dashed border appears beneath the mouse point. You'll also notice an insertion mark within the text in the form of a vertical line. This shows where the text would be inserted if you released the mouse button.

**6** If you are not happy with the order of the slides, you can reorder them. For ease, it's best to collapse all the slides first, so that you can see only their titles. Then select the slide you want to move by clicking on its icon and holding down the mouse button as you drag it to its new position. As you move the slide, the mouse pointer turns into a black four-headed arrow. PowerPoint also displays a horizontal black line on the Outline tab to indicate the slide's provisional new position. To insert the slide in the position shown, release the mouse button.

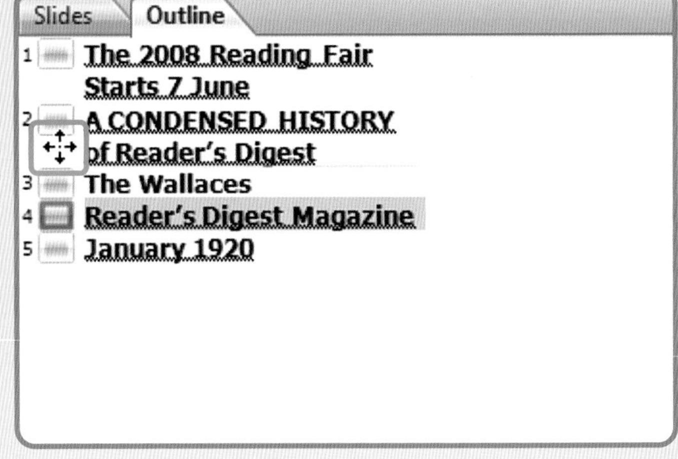

## Level adjustments

If you are working on a long presentation, try using the options in the Context menu, which is accessed by right-clicking on an item of text within the Outline tab. This reveals further options for redesigning your slides. For example, you can click on **Promote** or **Demote** to alter the level of a sub-category item. You can also collapse or expand text beneath the headings by clicking on **Collapse** or **Expand**.

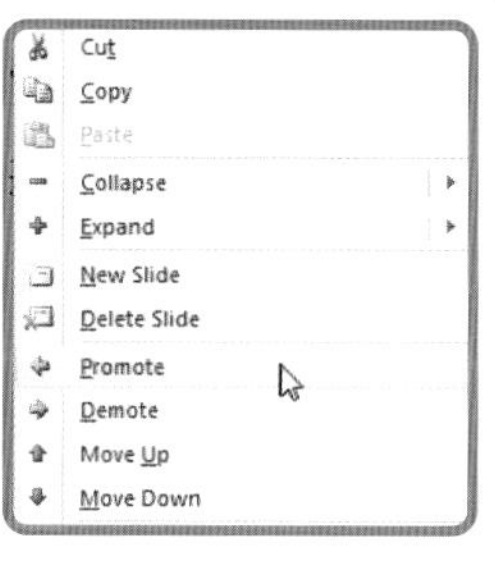


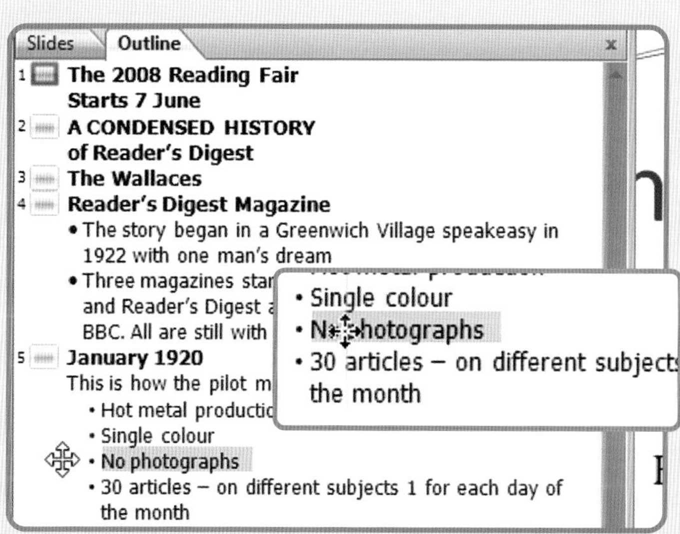


**7** You can also use the Outline tab to structure text within individual slides, allowing you, for example, to graphically separate main and sub-points. To indicate a sub-point, place the mouse pointer on the bullet before the relevant paragraph, hold down the mouse button and drag the text to the right. The mouse pointer turns into a black four-headed arrow. At the same time, a vertical line shows how much the text you are dragging will be indented when it is placed.

**8** Once you are satisfied, release the mouse button and you can see the change that has been made immediately in the main window. The program has indented the text and automatically reduced its font size in order to signify its relationship to the text above. The further you move text towards the right of the Outline tab, the more its font size is reduced. To add additional sub-points beneath an existing one, drag the new sub-points further to the right of the Outline than the existing one. To remove this new sub-division, drag the text back to its original position on the Outline tab.

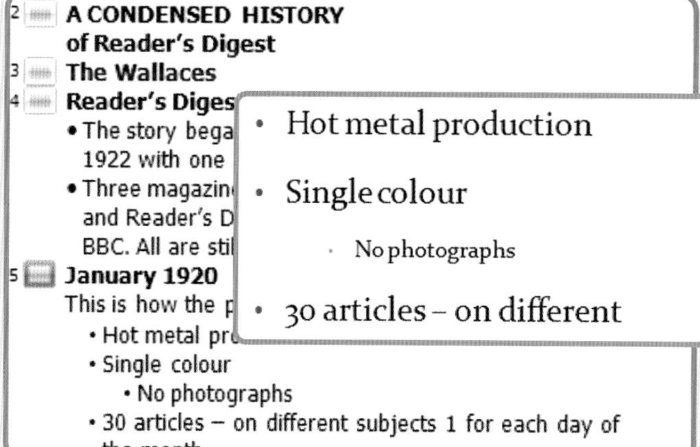

# Working with notes

Standing up and presenting to a group without a script to rely on can be nerve-racking. If nerves are a problem for you, it can be helpful to make notes to remind you of the key points in your presentation. PowerPoint's notes feature lets you add notes next to each slide which only you can see, and which can be printed out for future reference.


**SEE ALSO ...**

- *Print settings* p90
- *Slide shows* p92


**BEFORE YOU START**
*Start PowerPoint and create a presentation with several slides, or open an existing one. The notes pane is found beneath the main window in which the current slide is displayed.*

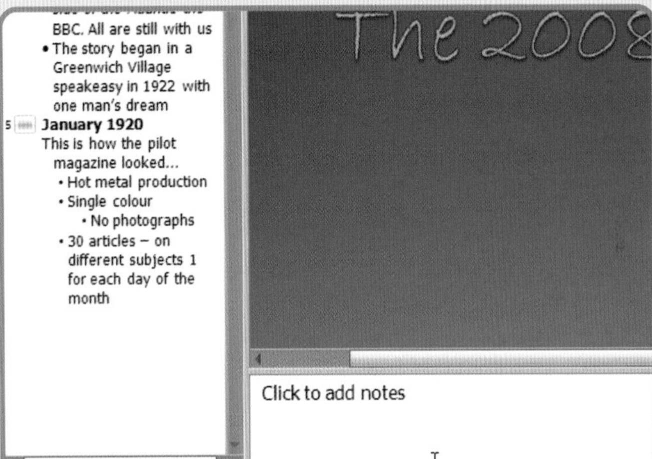


**1** The notes function in PowerPoint is designed to help the person giving the presentation. You can add reminders and comments to the pane as you create your individual slides. The advantage of this is that you have all the information you need to give a great presentation in the same document. Furthermore, the relationship between the notes and the slides to which they refer will be crystal clear from the moment you start work. Any text that you put in the notes pane is only visible to the person making the presentation.

**2** Click on the notes pane to remove the 'Click to add notes' text and type in your notes. If the notes pane is too small to show all your text, move the cursor above its upper edge, then click and drag to expand the pane. The notes are saved with the slides to which they refer. When you have finished the notes for the slide you are working on, use the overview in the Slides tab on the left of the screen, or the scroll bar on the right, to move to the next slide and enter the notes to go with it.

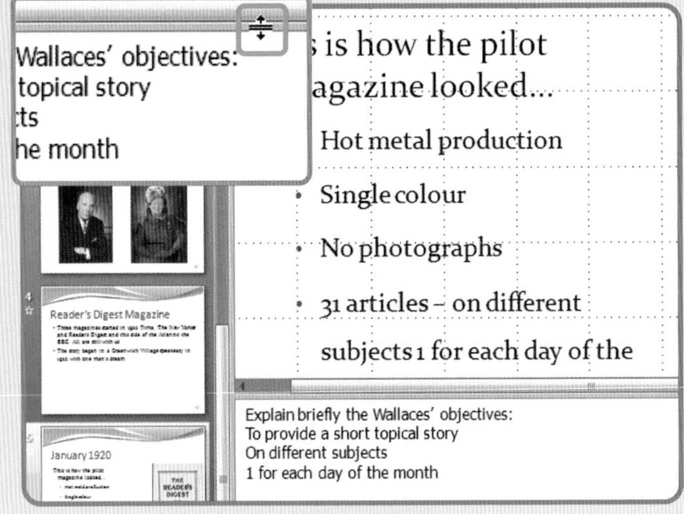

### Bright idea

***It's a good idea to emphasise particularly important points in your notes, and you can use all the usual formatting options to do so. For example, select a key term and click the* Bold *button in the Font group to make it stand out.***

### Expert advice

Keep your notes as brief and clear as you can. They should jog your memory, reminding you of the crucial points that you want to talk about. If you are not an experienced presenter use complete sentences rather than key words to make them easier to understand.

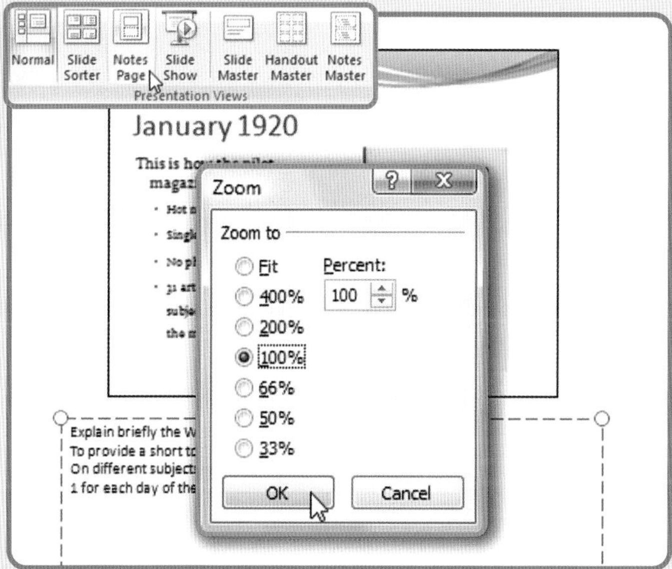


**3** If you prefer you can type notes in Print Preview. This shows how the presentation will look when you print both the slides and the notes together. Click on the **View** tab and choose **Notes Page** in the Presentation Views group. Write your notes in the box below the presentation slides. If the text is too small to read, click on **Zoom** in the Zoom group. Make your selection – 100% usually works well – and click on **OK**.

**4** To return to the original view, click on the **View** tab and then on **Normal** in the Presentation Views group. As the notes are only intended for the presenter and don't really form part of the actual presentation, you will need to select a special setting in order to print them out. Click on the **Office** button and select **Print** in the left pane. In the Print dialogue box, select **Notes Pages** from the 'Print what' drop-down menu.

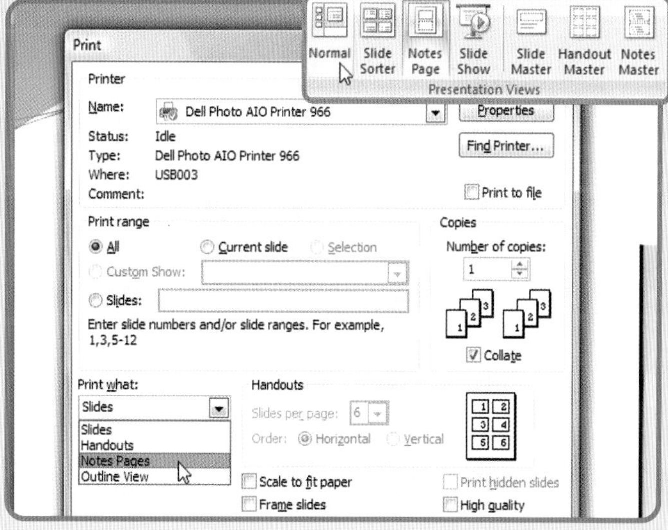

## That's amazing!

You can include pictures as well as text in your notes for a quick graphical reminder of a point that you need to make. To include an image in your notes, first click on the **View** tab and choose **Notes Page** in the Presentation Views group. Then click on the **Insert** tab and then on **Picture** to add the image. Use the sizing handles to adjust the size of the image and position it where you like.

## Close-up

***If your text is too small to read in Print Preview click your mouse anywhere on the page to enlarge the view. Click again to return to the previous setting.***

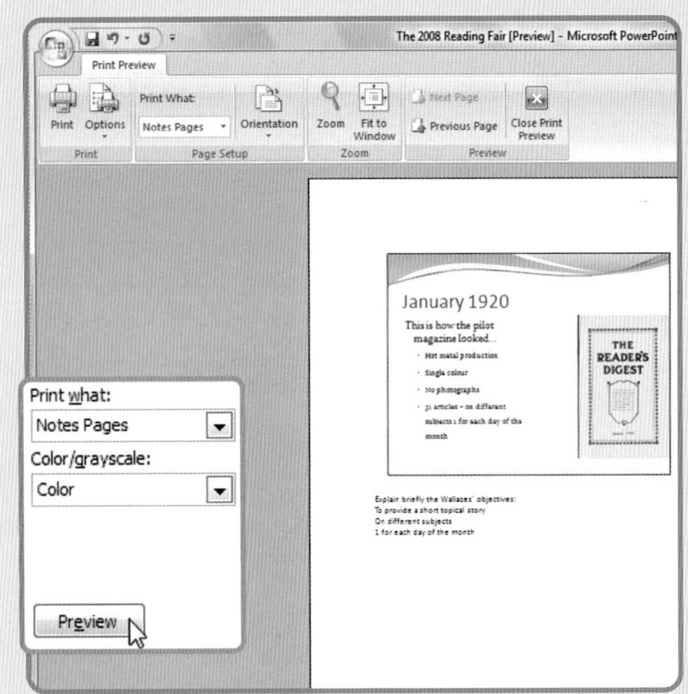


**5** Now click on the **Preview** button. The notes will be displayed just as they will look when you print them out. Click on **Next Page** and **Previous Page** in the Preview group to move through the slides.

**6** In many cases, the notes are easier to read when you print the pages in landscape rather than in the portrait format. To switch formats, click on **Orientation** in the Page Setup group. If you need to make further adjustments to the notes, click **Close Print Preview** in the Preview group to exit Print Preview and return to Normal view. Otherwise, click **Print** in the Print group and then, in the Print dialogue box, click on **OK** to start printing.

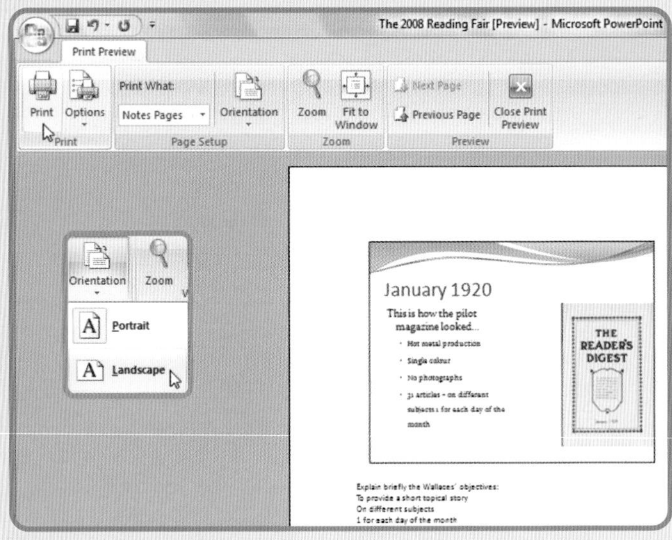

# Presentation Perfect

# Correcting mistakes

All the work you've put into a presentation can be spoilt by an error that you haven't noticed until you're giving your presentation. But PowerPoint's AutoCorrect feature can prevent this happening by detecting and correcting spelling mistakes and grammatical errors. You can even add your own common typographical errors to the list to be automatically corrected.

**SEE ALSO ...**

- *First steps* p20
- *Formatting text* p32

## ALL PRESENT AND CORRECT?

**PowerPoint's spell-checker will find your errors and suggest alternative spellings.**

### While you work

PowerPoint helps you to avoid errors in the text from the moment you start to create your presentation. Behind the scenes, it automatically checks every word as you type it. If the program finds a possible mistake, the offending word is highlighted on screen with a wavy red underline. Right-click on the word and – if available – choose one of the suggestions that PowerPoint offers to correct the error. You can reject PowerPoint's suggestions and, if you want to, add your own choice of word to the dictionary.

The spell-checker should be turned on by default. If it's not, click on the **Office** button and then on **PowerPoint Options**. Click on **Proofing** in the left pane and then in the third section of the right pane click to put a tick next to 'Check spelling as you type' and click on **OK** to confirm.

### When you've finished

You can leave the spell-checking until your presentation is finalised. Click on the **Review** tab then on **Spelling** in the Proofing group. In the

Spelling dialogue box, the 'Not in Dictionary' box gives the first spelling mistake that PowerPoint

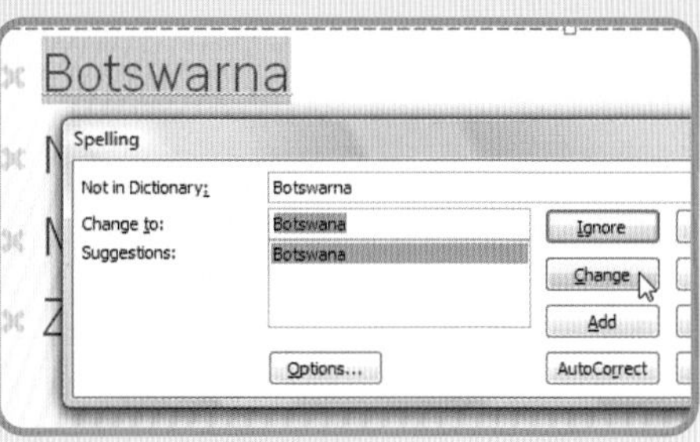

### Close-up

***The spell-checker is a very useful tool, but it won't automatically know every word in your presentation. You can improve the vocabulary contained in the built-in dictionary by adding words which the spell-checker has marked as incorrect but you know to be correct.***

### Bright idea

***You can use the AutoFormat feature to convert Internet addresses to hyperlinks so that when you click on the links during your presentation you will go straight to the Web sites in question. Hyperlinked text is blue and underlined (see page 100).***

has found. Click on **Change** or **Ignore** to accept or reject the suggested alternative, or add your own choice of word to the dictionary. When you have made your choice, the spell-checker will find the next error.

## STRAIGHT TO THE POINT

**Got the perfect word on the tip of your tongue? Reach for the PowerPoint Thesaurus.**

PowerPoint's Thesaurus helps you to find synonyms quickly. Right-click on the word you want to look up and choose **Synonyms** from the context menu. In the pane that opens up, click on one of the related words to insert it, or click on the **Thesaurus** in the Research task pane for further options.

## AUTOMATIC ERROR CORRECTION

**Depending on your settings, PowerPoint can also correct mistakes automatically.**

PowerPoint's AutoCorrect feature corrects common errors such as using two capital letters at the beginning of a word where you should use one, or starting sentences with a lower-case letter. You can customise the way AutoCorrect works by clicking on the **Office** button and then on **PowerPoint Options**. Click on **Proofing** in the left pane and then in the first section of the right pane click on **AutoCorrect Options**. The AutoCorrect English (United Kingdom) dialogue

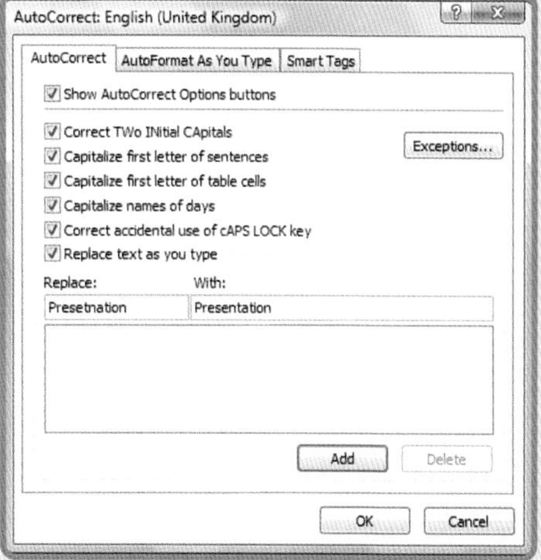


box appears. Click on the **AutoCorrect** tab. Add text that you frequently mistype in the 'Replace' area along with the correct typing in the 'With' area. If the 'Show AutoCorrect Options buttons' checkbox is ticked, PowerPoint draws a small blue

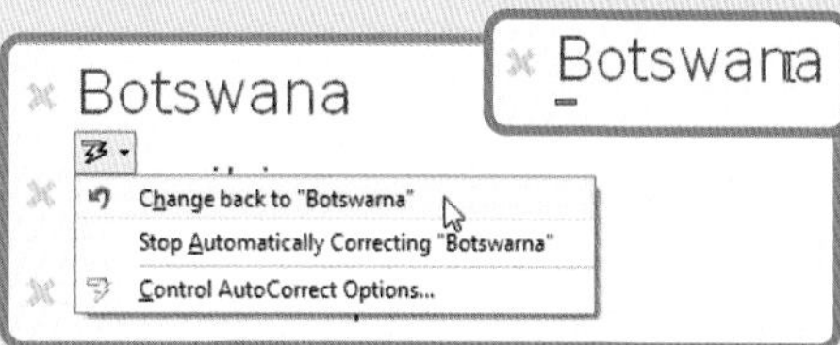


line underneath the first letter of every word it corrects. If you want to reverse a correction that PowerPoint has made, move the cursor over the blue line, click on the button that appears and choose from the options.

There may be words that you don't want to have automatically capitalised by the AutoCorrect

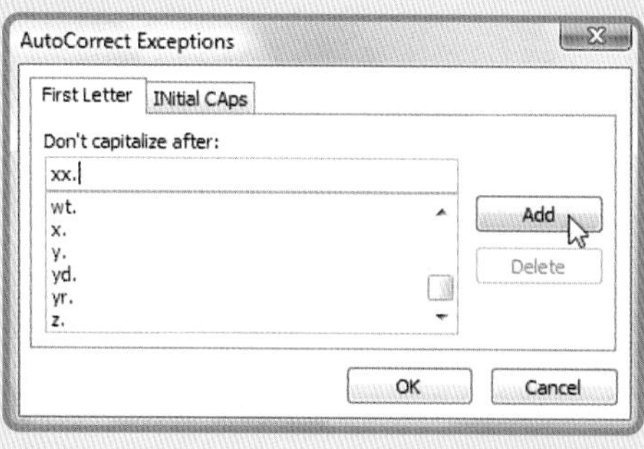


feature. If this is the case, click on the **Exceptions** button, type them into the box, click on **Add**, then click on **OK**.

The AutoFormat As You Type tab has options to enable you to identify and correct formatting

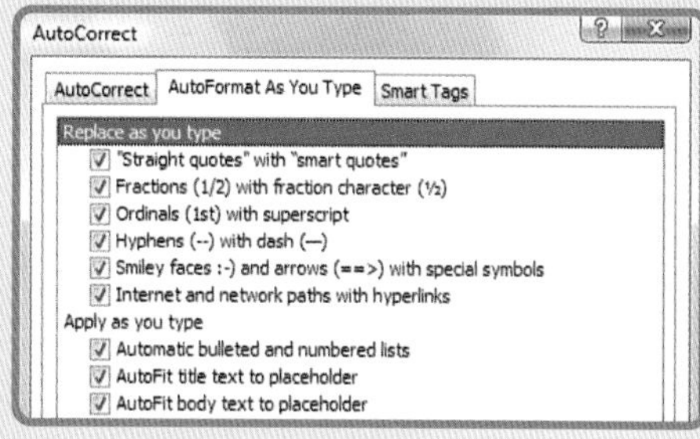


errors. Most of the formatting options found here are typographic embellishments such as automatically inserting quotation marks but there is also an option for turning Internet addresses into hyperlinks (see 'Bright idea', opposite).

### Watch out

Some of the changes you can make in the proofing options within PowerPoint, such as AutoCorrect, will affect other Office applications, including Word or Excel, if they are installed on your computer. So, you will need to make sure that your changes are acceptable in these programs as well.

# Transition effects

Give your slide show a professional touch by animating the transitions between slides. There are more than 50 different effects that can be applied to the process of moving from slide to slide. You aren't limited to one transition style for your entire presentation – you can choose a different effect for each slide and also vary the speed at which individual slides appear.


**SEE ALSO ...**

- *Animations* p86
- *Slide shows* p92
- *Recording a narration* p96


**BEFORE YOU START**

*Click on the **Office** button and then on **Open**. Select and open a presentation containing several slides. Click on the **View** tab and then on **Slide Sorter** in the Presentation Views group.*

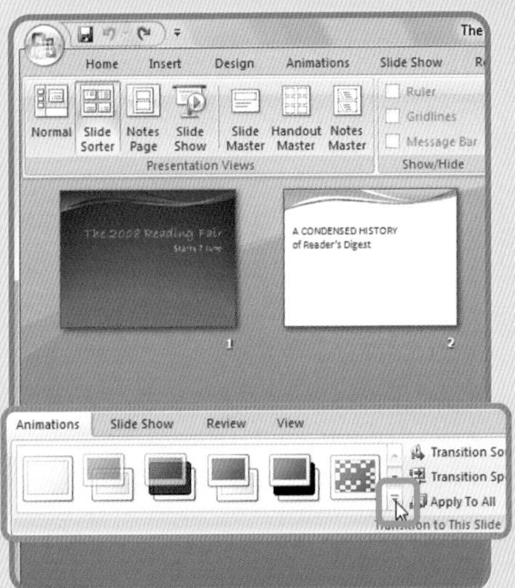


**1** In Slide Sorter view, select the slide to which you want to apply a transition effect. Click on the **Animations** tab, then click on a slide transition type in the Transition to This Slide group. To view more transition options, click on the **More** button found at the bottom right of the Transition to This Slide group.

**2** The drop-down menu contains transition effects grouped under 'Fades and Dissolves', 'Wipes', 'Push and Cover', 'Stripe and Bars' and 'Random'. Here we've chosen the 'Wedge' effect in the 'Wipes' group. PowerPoint displays a preview of the effect in Slide Sorter view. A star is added beneath a slide to indicate that a transition effect has been applied to it.

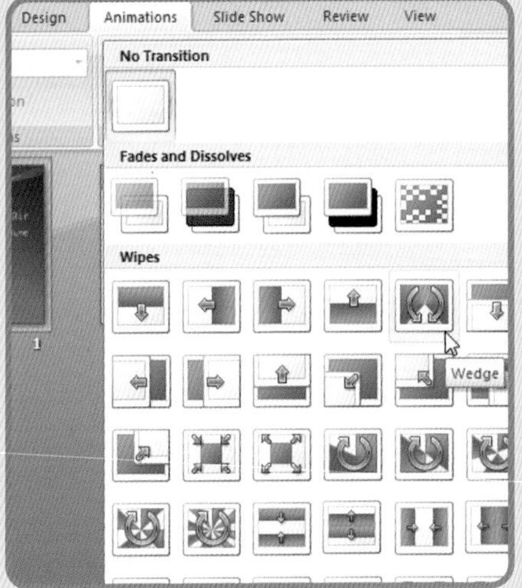

**3** To check that you are happy with the effect, click on the small star underneath the slide. To test the transition at full screen size, click the **Slide Show** button in the Presentation Views group. When you've finished, press the **Escape** key on the keyboard to return to Slide Sorter view. You'll probably need to experiment with the different transitions until you find one you're satisfied with.

### Bright idea

***If you want to set the same transition effect for every slide, choose the effect from the options in the Transitions to This Slide group and click on** Apply to All**.***

### That's amazing!

Using a different transition effect for each slide helps to add variety to your slide show – especially if it's a long presentation. PowerPoint can even decide which effect to use on your behalf. Scroll down to the bottom of the list in the Transition to This Slide drop-down menu and choose from the three options under 'Random'. Then click on **Apply to All Slides**. PowerPoint will choose a different transition effect for every slide in your presentation.

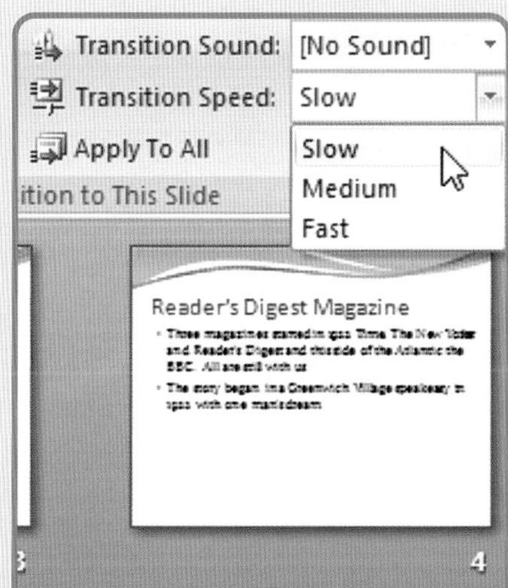


**4** You can adjust the effect further using the settings found to the right of the Transition to This Slide group. To change the speed at which the new slide is displayed on screen, for example, click on the 'Transition Speed' drop-down menu and choose an option (in this example, 'Slow' is selected).

**5** PowerPoint comes with sound effects that you can use in conjunction with the transition effects. They include applause, an explosion and a drum roll. To add a sound, click on the **Transition Sound** drop-down menu and choose an option – here it is 'Breeze'. Select **Other Sound** at the bottom of the menu to use a sound file you have created. Tick the 'Loop Until Next Sound' option to keep the sound running.

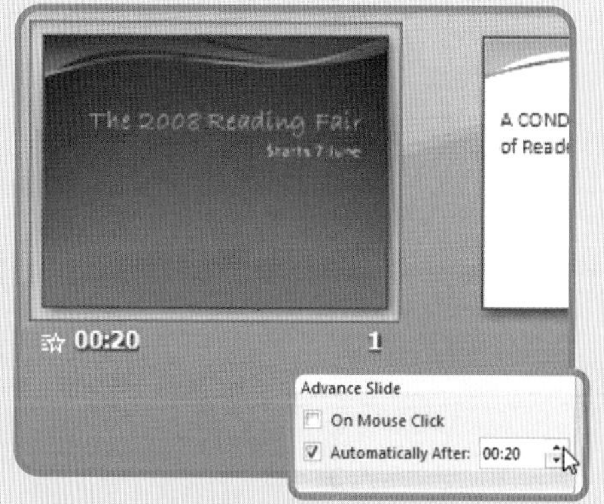


**6** On the far right of the Transition to This Slide group are options that allow you to set how long each slide in a slide show is displayed before the next one appears (see page 92). In the 'Advance slide' section, tick 'Automatically After' and enter a time in the box (in this example it's 20 seconds). The time you enter is shown underneath the respective slide in Slide Sorter view. To set the same time for multiple slides, ensure you are in Slide Sorter view, hold down the **Shift** key and select each slide in turn, then select a time.

# Animations

Another way to bring your presentation to life is to animate the text or shapes that are on your slides. PowerPoint has a wide variety of special effects available which allow you to make an object appear or disappear from a slide. These effects can also be used to highlight an element that is already on screen at a specific point in the presentation.

**SEE ALSO ...**

- *Transition effects* p84
- *Slide shows* p92

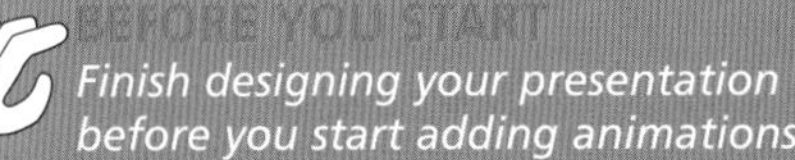

**BEFORE YOU START**

*Finish designing your presentation before you start adding animations.*

*Save the presentation and then select a slide to work on which contains a title, picture and a text box.*

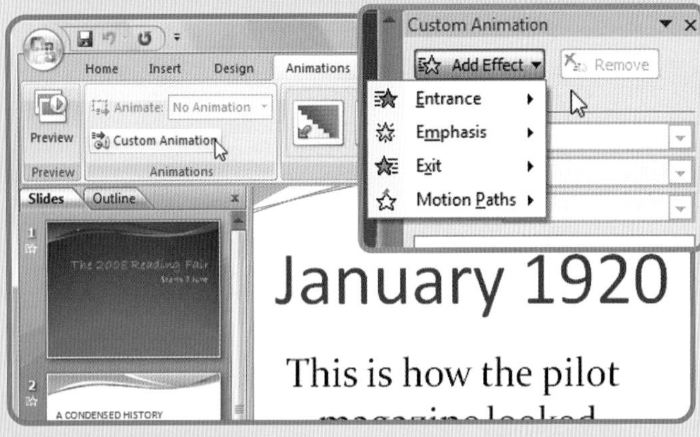


**1** Click on the **View** tab and then on **Normal** in the Presentation Views group. Then click on the **Animations** tab and choose **Custom Animation** in the Animations group. The Custom Animation task pane appears on the right of the window. You can animate an object you have selected by clicking on **Add Effect**. This opens a drop-down menu with sub-menus for four types of animation: 'Entrance' (effects used to make objects appear); 'Emphasis' (effects used to highlight objects at a given time); 'Exit' (effects used to remove objects from the screen) and 'Motion Paths' (effects used to move objects around the slide). In the following steps, the objects will be displayed one by one, gradually filling up the slide.

**2** To animate the slide title, for example, ensure it is selected, then click on **Add Effect**, select **Entrance** and then **Blinds**. PowerPoint applies the animation and plays a preview in the document window (see 'Bright idea', opposite). A number in a small box appears at the top left of the object (here, it's number '1' because it is the first animation to be applied). The effect is also listed in the task pane with its corresponding number.

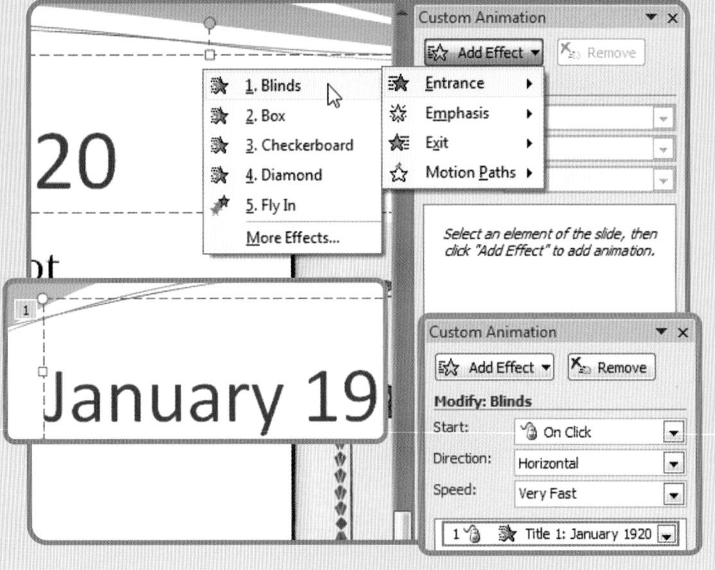

### Expert advice

The menus that appear when you click on the 'Add Effect' button only include a handful of the available effects. To see the complete list, choose **More Effects** and select from the options in the dialogue box. PowerPoint displays a preview of the effect in the main document window. If the preview blocks from view the object that you are animating, click on the Title Bar of the dialogue box and drag and drop it in a different position on the screen.

### Bright idea

***If the AutoPreview checkbox in the Custom Animation task pane is ticked, PowerPoint automatically previews an effect as soon as you add or modify it. You can run the effect again at any time by clicking either the*** *Play* ***or*** *Slide Show* ***buttons, found in the Custom Animation task pane.***

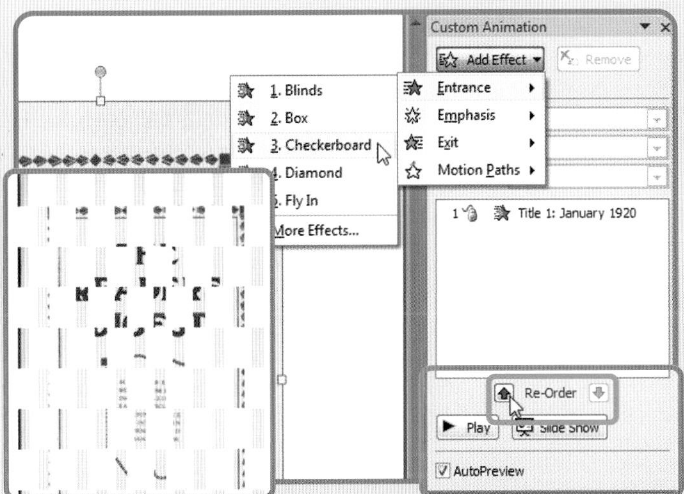


**3** Animating pictures works in the same way as text. Select the picture, click on **Add Effect** and choose an effect, (here, we've chosen 'Entrance' and then 'Checkerboard'. The picture is marked with a small number '2', and the effect is added to the list in the task pane. When you present the slide show, the animations run in the order in which they appear in this list, starting at number 1. To change the order, click on an effect in the task pane and then click on one of the arrow buttons next to 'Re-Order' to move it up or down in the order.

**4** You can customise when the animations will appear. First, select an animation in the task pane. If you want the effect to run when you click the mouse during your slide show, select **On Click** in the 'Start' drop-down menu. The 'With Previous' option makes the new animation run at the same time as the previous one in the list, while the 'After Previous' option runs the animation as soon as the previous effect has finished. The 'Direction' and 'Speed' drop-down menus let you control how the animation appears on the slide.

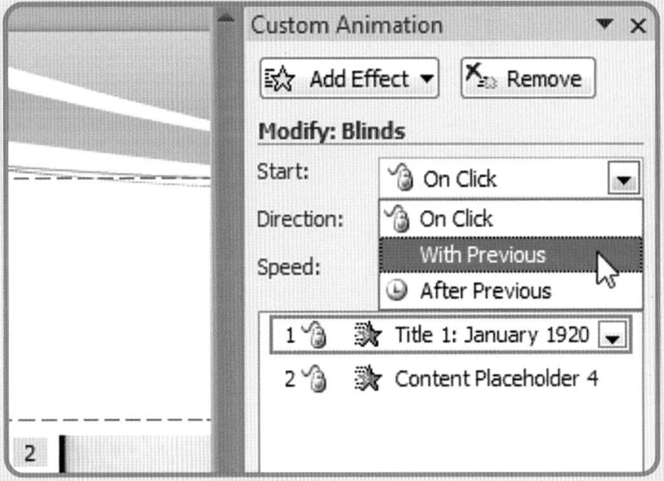

### That's amazing!

You can attribute more than one effect to a particular object at the same time. So you can use, for example, an 'Entrance' effect of 'Checkerboard' and an 'Exit' effect of 'Diamond'.

### Changing and removing effects

It is possible to substitute an effect with another effect at a later point. Just highlight the effect you'd like to replace in the task pane and click on the **Change** button. The drop-down menu that opened in Step 1 will now appear. Click on a new effect to replace the existing one. To delete an effect completely, click on **Remove**.

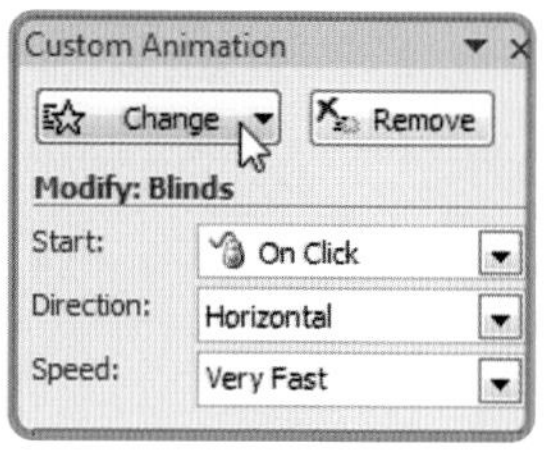


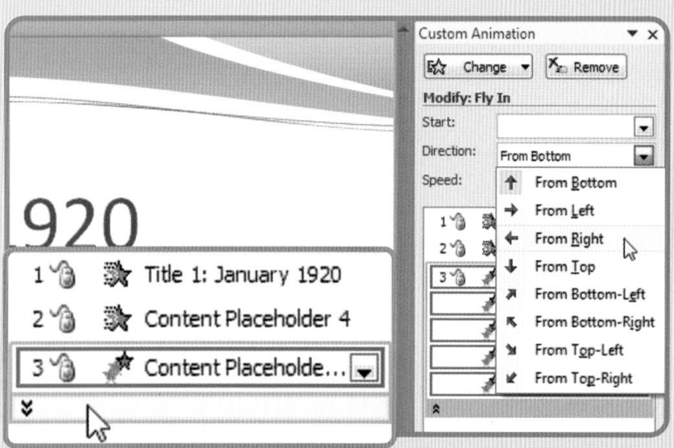


**5** Now select the text box, click on **Add Effect** and choose an effect (here, we've chosen 'Entrance' followed by 'Fly In'). If, as in this example, the text box contains a list, the animation effect is applied to each item in the list individually (in this example effect numbers 3-7). However, in the task pane all the effects are shown as one animation, stored under effect number 3. This means that adjustments like those made in Step 4 will be applied to all the items in the list. If you want to give different effects to each entry, click on the arrow to expand the list and click on the effect you want to adjust. Use the options in the 'Start', 'Direction' and 'Speed' menus to customise the effect.

**6** You can make additional adjustments to an effect by right-clicking on it in the task pane and choosing **Effect Options** from the context menu. The options shown in the dialogue box that appears depend on the effect selected. Under the 'Effect' tab, you can specify the direction that the 'Fly In' effect appears from. Under 'Enhancements', the 'Sound' drop-down menu allows you to play a sound-effect with the animation (here it is 'Applause') and the 'Animate text' drop-down menu lets you choose whether the effect is applied to complete words or to individual characters. Click on **OK** to confirm your choices.

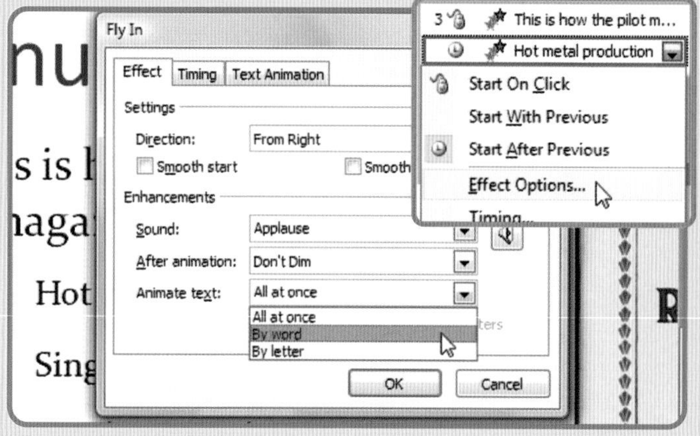

## Close-up

***When you present a slide show, effects are normally activated by clicking the mouse or pressing a key such as the Spacebar – just like moving to the next slide. It is important to remember that if you have applied a separate entry effect to a list, you'll need to activate each item on the list in turn (see opposite).***

## Expert advice

There are several ways to select multiple slides in Slide Sorter view. To select all the slides, make sure that the Home tab is selected, then click on **Select** in the Editing group and choose **Select All** from the drop-down menu, or press **Ctrl** + **A** on your keyboard. To select multiple, non-consecutive slides, click each one in turn while holding down the **Ctrl** key. To select a series of consecutive slides, click on the first slide, hold down the **Shift** key and click the last slide.

**7** You can combine effects with transitions. Open a presentation, and click on an object, here a bulleted list. Click on the **Animations** tab, then click on the 'Animate' drop-down menu in the Animations group. The menu displays three default animations: 'Fade' (where objects appear gradually); 'Wipe' (where objects appear from their bottom point up) and 'Fly In' (where objects move in from the side of the screen). Below each, you can choose to bring in the object in one go, 'All At Once', or if it is a list, you can bring it in line by line, 'By 1st Level Paragraphs'. Click on your choice to select it.

**8** PowerPoint applies the animation scheme to the object in that slide and runs a preview of the effects. To repeat the preview, click on the little star underneath the slide in the Slides pane. To apply a different scheme to the object, make sure that it is still selected, and click on the arrow to access the options for 'Animate' as in Step 7. Make a different selection from the drop-down menu. To remove a scheme, click on **No Animation** in the 'Animate' drop-down menu.

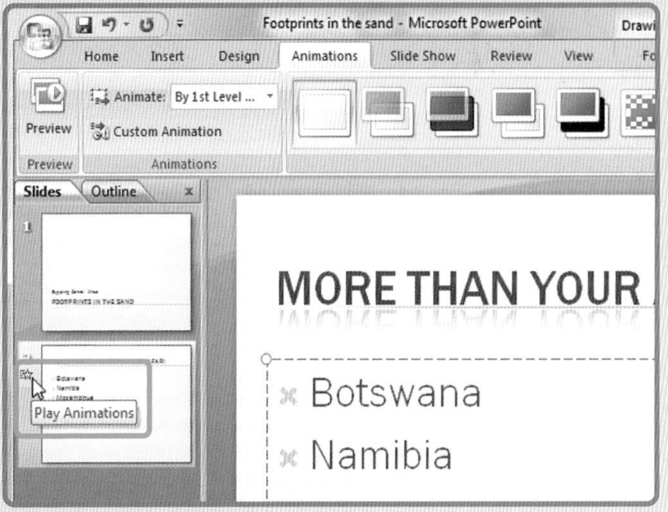

# Print settings

In PowerPoint, there's more to printing than meets the eye. Open the Print dialogue box and you will be presented with a range of options that allow you to print your presentation exactly the way you need it. Whether you want to print in black and white or full colour, with each slide on a page of its own or with multiple slides on one page, the choice is yours.

**SEE ALSO ...**

- *Presenting & printing* p28
- *Working with notes* p78
- *Slide shows* p92

## PRINTING PRESENTATIONS

**The first step is to open the Print dialogue box. This can be done by clicking on the** Office Button **and choosing** Print, **or by clicking on a Desktop shortcut or an icon on the Quick Access Toolbar.**

### Standard settings

As with most other Office programs, there are a few settings you'll need to check before you print. If you have more than one printer attached to your computer, make sure the correct printer is chosen. The printers installed on your machine are listed in the 'Name' drop-down menu. Click on **Properties** to adjust the page orientation and any settings specific to your printer, such as the paper size.

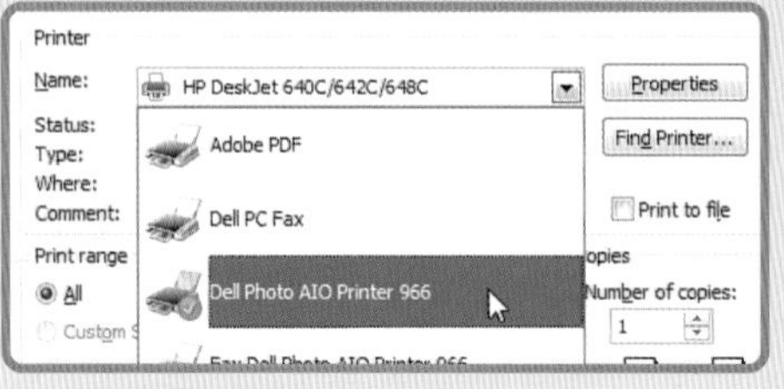


### What will be printed?

You can choose to print the whole presentation or just a few slides. The relevant settings are found in the 'Print range' area of the Print dialogue box.

By default the Print range is set to 'All'. You can, however, choose to print only the current slide or certain slides. To print the current slide, click on the radio button next to 'Current slide'. To print specific slides by slide number or by a range of slide numbers, click the 'Slides' radio button and enter the slide numbers in the adjacent box. Separate each slide number with a comma and use a hyphen to indicate a range of consecutive slides. If you have set up several slide shows from one presentation (see page 94) you can also specify which version to print. It is also possible to print hidden slides (see page 94).

Print range
All | Current slide | Selection
Custom Show:
Slides: 1,3,5
Enter slide numbers and/or slide ranges. For example, 1,3,5-12
Copies
Number of copies: 1
Collate

### How many copies?

If you're confident that there are no mistakes in your presentation, you can print off as many copies as you need in one go. Enter the number of copies required in the 'Copies' area. To collate the pages in complete sets, tick the 'Collate' checkbox.

### Watch out

If you are printing in greyscale, you may find that text positioned on a coloured background is hard to read. If so, you'll need to adjust the theme colour (see page 53).

### Bright idea

*If you want to produce multiple high-quality printed copies of your presentation, it may work out cheaper, particularly if you are using an inkjet printer, to print off one copy and then make photocopies of it.*

## How will the presentation be printed?

You can specify exactly how you want your presentation to be printed. PowerPoint gives you four different options in the 'Print what' drop-down menu. Choose 'Slides' to print each slide at actual size or choose 'Handouts' to print miniature versions of multiple slides on one sheet. If you select the latter you can use the options in the 'Handouts' area to specify the number of slides shown on each sheet and whether they are arranged horizontally or vertically across the page. Alternatively, you can print the 'Outline View' of your presentation, which means that you will see the headings of each slide in a list, or just the 'Notes Pages'.

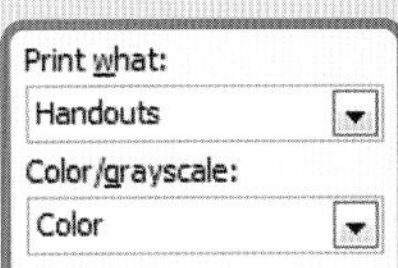


There are also options to let you scale the printout to fit the paper size you are using, print a frame around the slides and include any comments and handwritten notes added during a slide show on the printout. If you have a colour printer, you can also choose whether to print in greyscale or colour.

## PRINT PREVIEW

**Take a close look at your slides and check that all the settings are correct before you send them to the printer.**

When you have set all the print options, click on **Preview** to have a final look at the presentation and make sure that you have selected all the options correctly.

The first slide of your printout appears in a new window that fills the screen area. If you need to, you can make adjustments to the print settings by clicking on the options on the Ribbon. The 'Print What' drop-down menu, for example, gives you another chance to choose between printing out the presentation as 'Slides', 'Handouts', 'Outline View' and 'Notes Pages'.

You can put the date, time and slide number on your printouts. To do this, click on the **Options** button, select **Header and Footer** and in the dialogue box that appears tick the elements you want to include and decide where they should go. Make your final adjustments, then click on **Apply** or **Apply to All**, as appropriate.

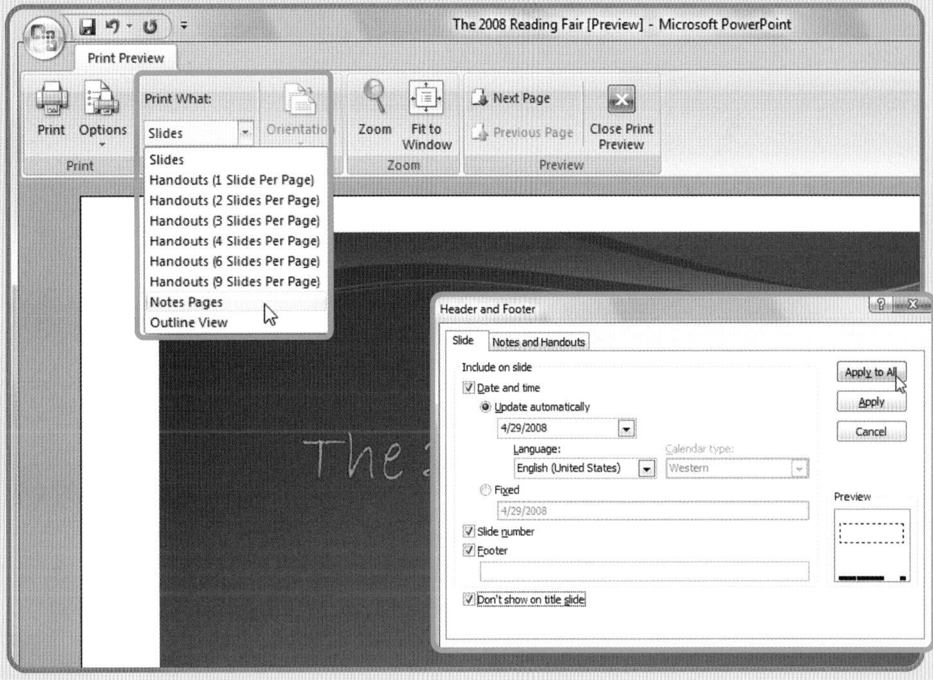


### Expert advice

If you select 'Handouts' from the 'Print what' options in the Print dialogue box, and choose to print 3 slides per page, a number of blank lines are placed either below or to the right of each slide (depending on your page orientation), for your audience to take notes.

### Close-up

***To enlarge Print Preview, click anywhere on the slide. Use the*** *Previous Page* ***and*** *Next Page* ***buttons in the Preview group to move to the Previous and Next slides, or press the*** *Page Up* ***and*** *Page Down* ***keys on the keyboard.***

# Slide shows

With a little bit of planning, you will soon be able to show your presentation to an audience on screen or using a projector. Exactly how and what you present is entirely up to you. Using the Slide Show options, you can set up your presentation to be presented by a speaker, controlled by the person viewing the presentation or to run automatically.

**SEE ALSO ...**

- *Using sounds* p66
- *Transition effects* p84
- *Animations* p86

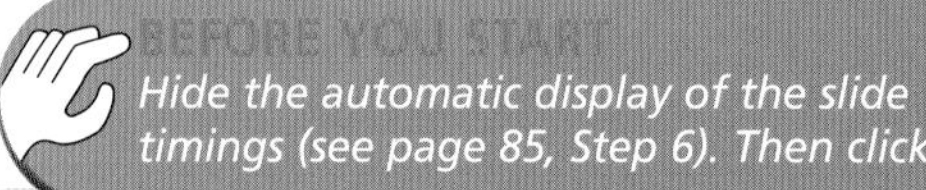

BEFORE YOU START
*Hide the automatic display of the slide timings (see page 85, Step 6). Then click on the* ***Slide Show*** *tab on the Ribbon and click on* ***Set Up Slide Show*** *in the Set Up group.*

Set Up Show
Show type
Presented by a speaker (full screen)
Browsed by an individual (window)
Show scrollbar
Browsed at a kiosk (full screen)

**1** The Set Up Show dialogue box lets you choose how to present your slide show. Click on the radio button next to 'Presented by a speaker (full screen)' to display the presentation using the full screen area and give the speaker control of the slides. If you choose 'Browsed by an individual (window)' a toolbar appears with options that allow the viewer to move from slide to slide. If you select 'Browsed at a kiosk (full screen)', you'll need to set the timings for how long each slide is displayed on screen. This is an automatic slide show which will repeat until you press the **Escape** key.

**2** You'll find additional settings in the 'Show options' section. Tick the 'Loop continuously until 'Esc'' checkbox to make PowerPoint repeat the presentation continuously. If you have recorded a narration (see page 96) and you do not want it to be heard, you can prevent it from playing by ticking the 'Show without narration' checkbox. Similarly, you can suppress effects you have set up by ticking the 'Show without animation' checkbox.

Show options
Loop continuously until 'Esc'
Show without narration
Show without animation
Pen color:
Performance
Use hardware graphics acceleration

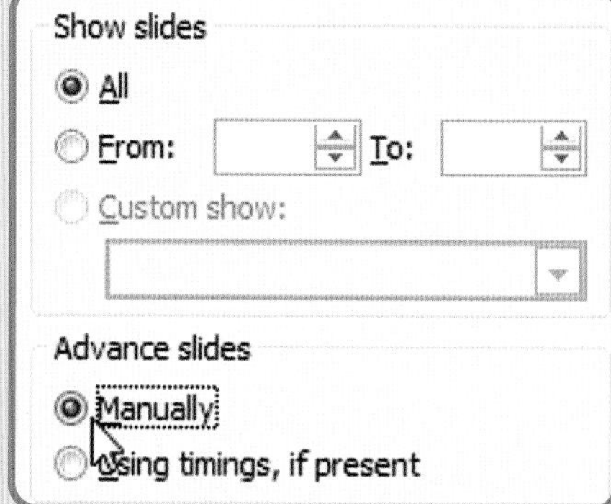


**3** The 'Show slides' section allows you to select which slides to include in the slide show. Select 'From ... To' and enter the slide numbers in the boxes, or choose an option from the 'Custom show' drop-down menu (see 'Expert advice', page 94). You can set how the slide show goes to the next slide in the 'Advance slides' panel. Choose 'Manually' to move to the next slide by clicking the mouse or pressing a key, or choose 'Using timings, if present' to use the timings set in the 'Slide Transition' task pane (see page 85). Click on **OK**.

**Bright idea**

***It's always worth doing a few practice runs before you present your slide show in front of an audience. That way, you'll boost your confidence about giving the presentation and you can iron out any problems that crop up.***

### Keyboard shortcuts

Mastering a few keyboard shortcuts will help you to guide your audience through your presentation smoothly. Often, several keys will fulfil the same purpose.

To go to the next slide or outline point: **Return** key or **Spacebar** or **Page Down.**
To go back to the previous slide or outline point: **Backspace** or **Page Up.**
To go to the first slide: **1** followed by the **Return** key.
To go to any slide: Slide number followed by the **Return** key.
To show or hide a black screen: **B** or **.**.
To show or hide a white screen: **W** or **,**.
To stop or restart an automatic slide show: **S** or **+**.
To delete handwritten notes: **E**.
To end the slide show: **Esc** or **–**.

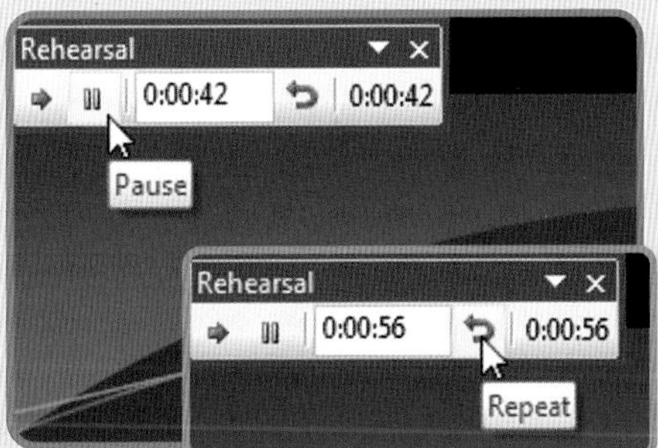


**4** It is also possible to set the time needed for each slide to be screened in a test run. This is very useful when you want to match the display times to a speaker's script. Select the **Slide Show** tab and click on **Rehearse Timings** in the Set Up group. PowerPoint starts a slide show and displays the Rehearsal toolbar. Run through your presentation at the speed you will be giving it, clicking the mouse or pressing a key whenever you are ready to move to the next slide. If you need to take a break, click the **Pause** button. To start your rehearsal of a slide again, click on **Repeat**.

**5** At the end of your presentation, a dialogue box appears showing how long the test run took. To accept the timing, click on **Yes**. Click on the **View** tab, then on **Slide Sorter** in the Presentation views group. You'll find the time taken for each slide displayed underneath the slide thumbnails. To apply these times to the slide show, click on **Set Up Slide Show** in the Set Up group and, in the 'Advance slides' section of the dialogue box, tick the 'Using timings, if present' checkbox.

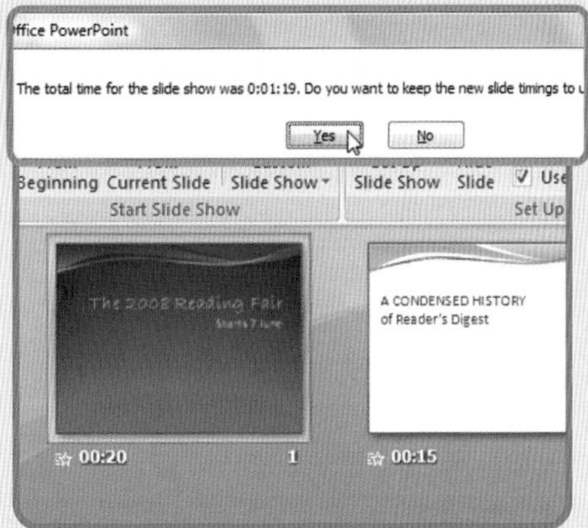


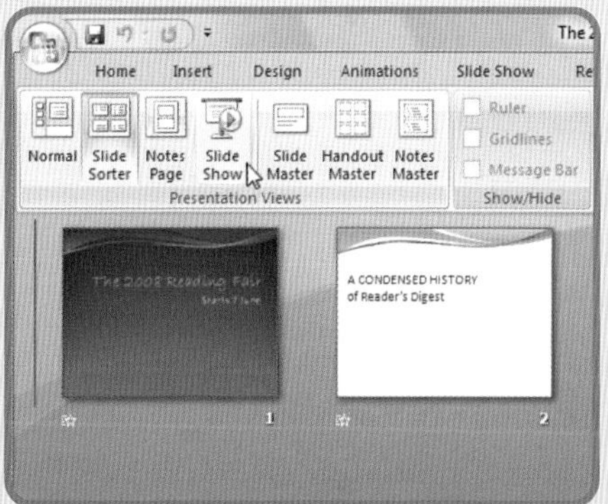


**6** The next few steps apply only to presentations given by a speaker moving through the slides manually. To start the slide show, click on the **View** tab if it's not already selected, and then click on **Slide Show** in the Presentation Views group, or press **F5** on your keyboard. PowerPoint displays the first slide and pauses. Click the mouse or, if you have one, use the scroll wheel to display the next slide or paragraph. Better still, use keyboard shortcuts (see box above) to move through the slides.

## Expert advice

You can use PowerPoint to create different versions of a presentation to show to different audiences. Click on the **Slide Show** tab and in the Start Slide Show group click on **Custom Slide Shows**, then **Custom Shows**. Then click on **New**. A dialogue box appears, allowing you to add slides to your new version. Click on a slide in the left panel then on the **Add** button to add it to the 'Custom Show' panel on the right. Click on **OK** to finish. Repeat these steps to create as many different versions as you need. You can then select the version you want to present using the Set Up Show dialogue box (see Step 3).

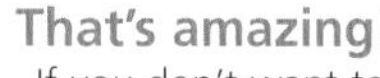

## That's amazing!

If you don't want to show the whole presentation, you can temporarily hide some of the slides. Select the Slide Sorter view and click on the **Slide Show** tab. Select the slides you don't want to present and click on **Hide Slide** in the Set Up group. In Slide Sorter view, the numbers of the hidden slides are now crossed out. To show a hidden slide again, repeat the steps you used to hide it.

**7** The mouse pointer is automatically hidden during a slide show. If you move the mouse, however, the mouse pointer appears accompanied by four very faint symbols in the bottom left corner of the screen. The arrow buttons on the left and right take you to the previous and next slides respectively, while the middle two buttons each conceal a menu. Click on the 'Pen' icon to write handwritten annotations on the slide. 'The Felt Tip Pen' and 'Highlighter' options are perfect for underlining and emphasising your points.

**8** Select **Felt Tip Pen**, for example, and the mouse pointer turns into a pen tip which you can use to draw directly onto the slide. To remove your annotations, press the **E** key on your keyboard. You can access more options by clicking on the slide symbol in the bottom left corner of the screen or by right-clicking anywhere on the slide. The **Go to Slide** option, for example, lets you go straight to any slide in the presentation.

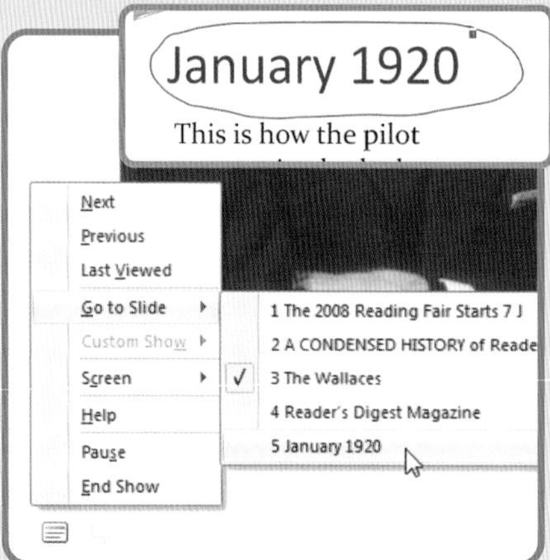


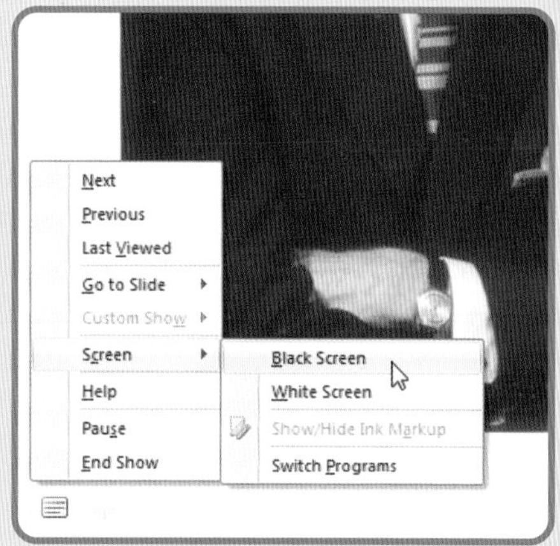


**9** To interrupt the presentation, click on the slide symbol in the bottom left corner of the screen, select the **Screen** option and choose **Black Screen** or **White Screen** (they are the same but the white screen can be written on with the felt tip pen). Return to the presentation by clicking on the slide symbol and choosing **Unblack Screen**. To interrupt timed slide shows, choose **Pause**. To finish the slide show, click on **End Show** or press the **Escape** key.

# Advanced Techniques

# Recording a narration

It's not always possible or necessary for a speaker to give a presentation in person. For instance, when a project needs to be shown repeatedly over the course of a day, it is best to run it as an automated slide show. Even if you're not there to present the slide show in person, you can still explain the slides to your audience by adding a recorded narration.

**SEE ALSO ...**
- *Using sounds* p66
- *Slide shows* p92

**BEFORE YOU START**
*Make sure you have a microphone and speakers connected to your computer and switched on. Click on the **Office** button, then on **Open** and select your presentation.*

**1** The first step is to write your narration. Go through the slides in turn and create some text for each one. For testing purposes, you'll want to move through the slides in the presentation manually by clicking the mouse. To set this up, click on the **Animations** tab and then in the Advance Slide panel of the Transition to This Slide group, tick the 'On Mouse Click' checkbox and make sure that the 'Automatically After' checkbox is not ticked. Then click on **Apply to All**.

**2** Now print out your script and check that you can read through it without making any errors. Click the mouse to move to the next slide as you read through your narration. Before you start recording, make sure that your microphone is turned on and set up correctly. Click on the **Slide Show** tab, and then on **Record Narration** in the Set Up group. In the Record Narration dialogue box click on **Set Microphone Level**.

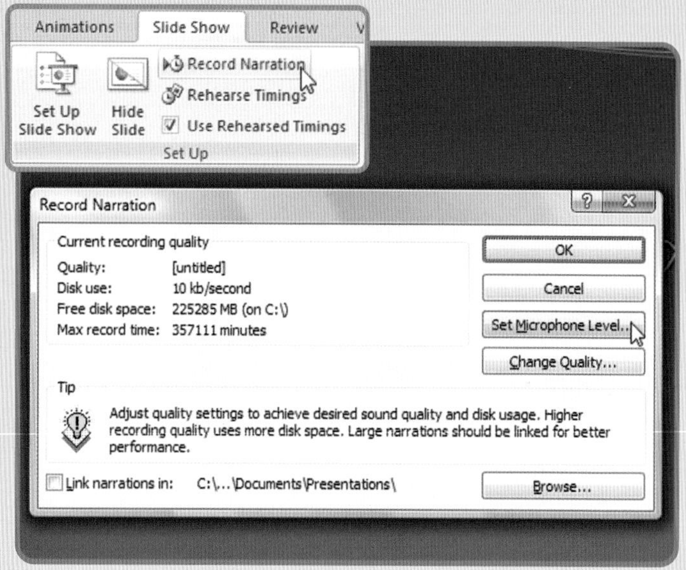

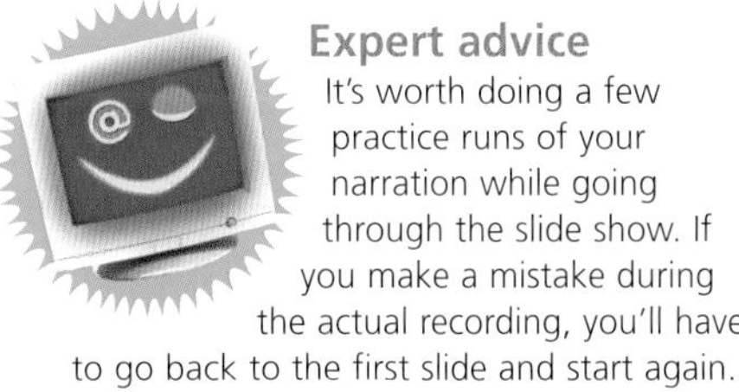

**Expert advice**

It's worth doing a few practice runs of your narration while going through the slide show. If you make a mistake during the actual recording, you'll have to go back to the first slide and start again.

**Bright idea**

***The quickest way to switch between PowerPoint and another application is to hold down the*** *Windows* ***key and then press the*** *Tab* ***key. Windows will display the icons of all open programs with the icon of the program that is currently active at the front. Keep pressing the*** *Tab* ***key until the program you want is at the front, and then release the Windows key.***

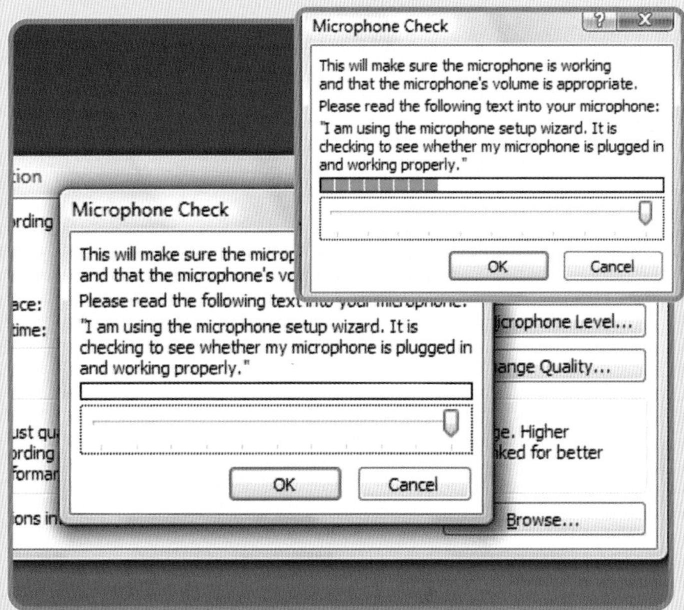


**3** In the Microphone Check dialogue box perform the test as described to ensure that the recording levels are set correctly. As you start speaking into the microphone a green line indicates that the microphone is working and also gives the sound level of your narration. Click on **OK** to finish.

**4** If the sound quality is not acceptable click on the **Change Quality** button. This displays the Sound Selection dialogue box. Use the 'Name' drop-down menu to choose between three quality levels: 'Radio Quality', 'Telephone Quality' and 'CD Quality'. 'CD Quality' is the best option, but it takes up the most disk space. Click **OK** to confirm your choice.

In the 'Current recording quality' section of the Record Narration dialogue box, 'Max record time' tells you how many minutes of narration you have space to record on your hard drive.

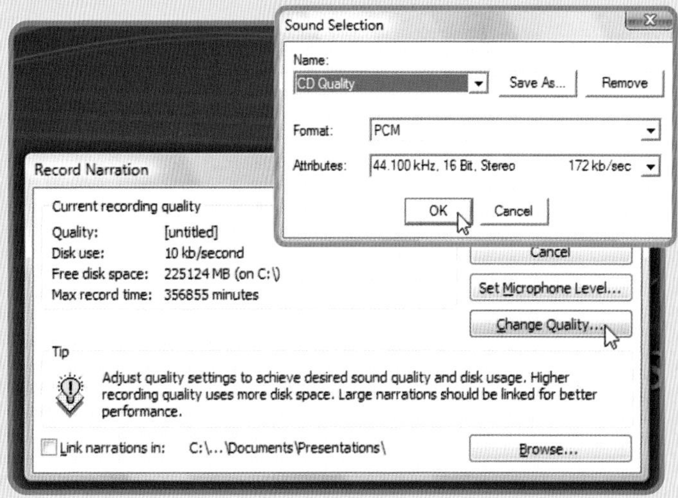

## Taking a break

If it is a longer presentation it's often necessary when recording a commentary to pause briefly, in order to clear your throat or take a sip of water. If this is the case, right-click your mouse and choose **Pause Narration** in the context menu. To continue the presentation right-click again and choose **Resume Narration**.

## Watch out

If your presentation contains animation which starts on a mouse click, don't forget when recording the narration to include this mouse click. Otherwise your presentation will lose its timing.

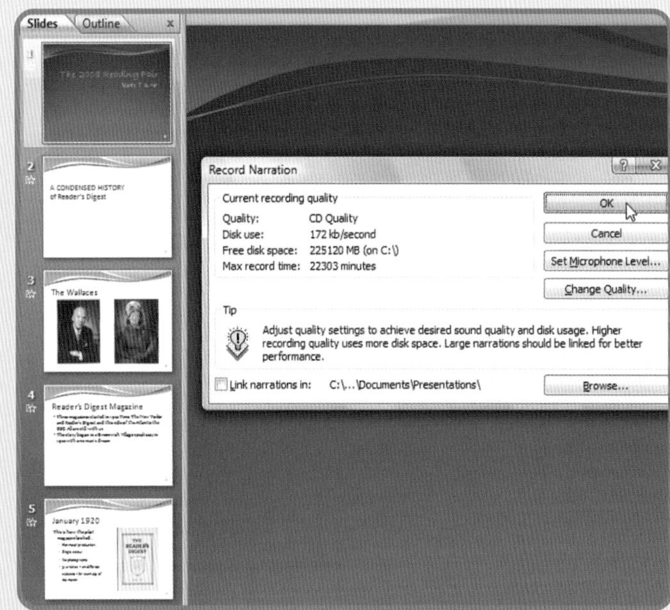


**5** Make sure that the first slide is selected in the Slides tab on the left of the screen. Then click on **OK** in the Record Narration dialogue box to start recording the narration. The recording will begin immediately. Read out your narration, clicking the mouse each time you need to move to the next slide.

**6** When you have finished the recording, PowerPoint asks if you want to save the timings you recorded for each slide. If you save the timings, each slide will be shown for exactly the same length of time as it takes to play the relevant part of your narration. Click on **Save**. An overview of the slides appears showing the length of the commentary for each slide beneath each of the slide thumbnails. To carry on working on your presentation, click on the **View** tab and then click on **Normal** in the Presentation Views group.

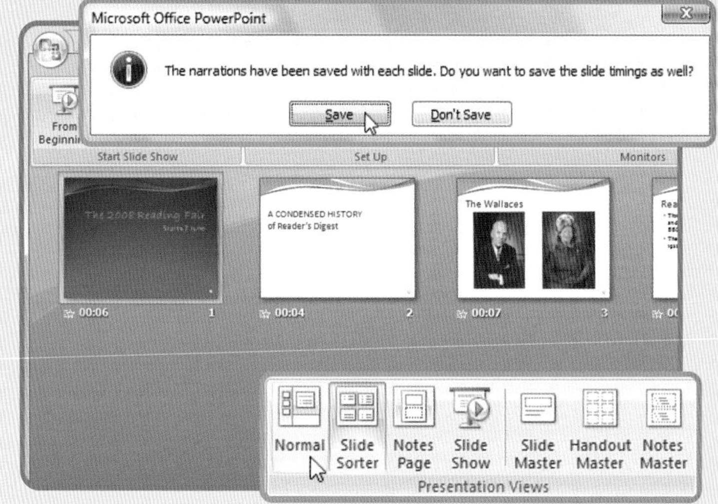

## Expert advice

If you set your slide show to loop continuously, it's a good idea to insert an extra slide at the end with a message that the presentation is over. That way, it is clear when your presentation starts and finishes.

## Bright idea

***If you decide to give your presentation in person after all, you will need to turn off the recorded narration. To do this, click on the*** *Slide Show* ***tab and then on*** *Set Up Slide Show*. ***In the dialogue box that appears, tick the 'Show without narration' checkbox and then click on*** *OK* ***to close the dialogue box again.***

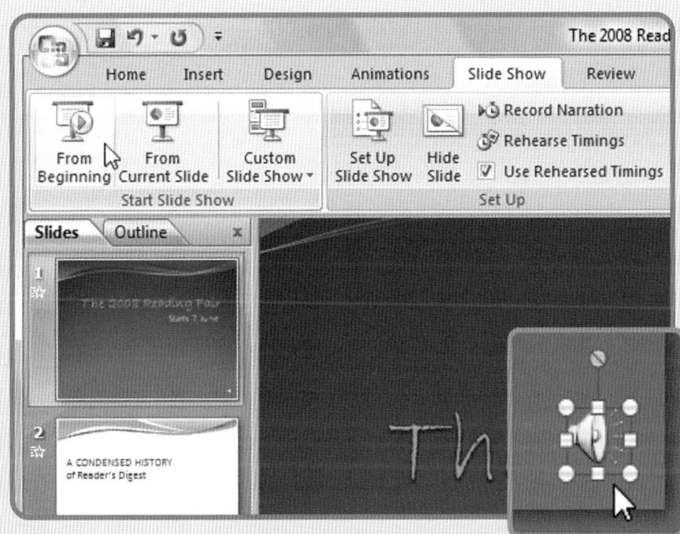


**7** To check the narration, make sure your loudspeaker is switched on, click on the **Slide Show** tab and choose **From Beginning** in the Start Slide Show group (or press **F5** on your keyboard). If you made a mistake during the recording, you'll need to delete it and start again. Select the loudspeaker icon in the bottom right-hand corner of the slide by clicking on it and then press the **Delete** key. Do this on every slide before repeating Steps 5 and 6 to make a new recording.

**8** If you want the slide show to repeat automatically after the last slide, click on the **Slide Show** tab and then on **Set Up Slide Show** in the Set Up group. In the 'Show type' panel at the top left of the Set Up Show dialogue box that appears, select the 'Browsed at a kiosk (full screen)' option. Click on **OK** to confirm the setting. Once started, the slide show will run in a continuous loop until you press the **Esc** key.

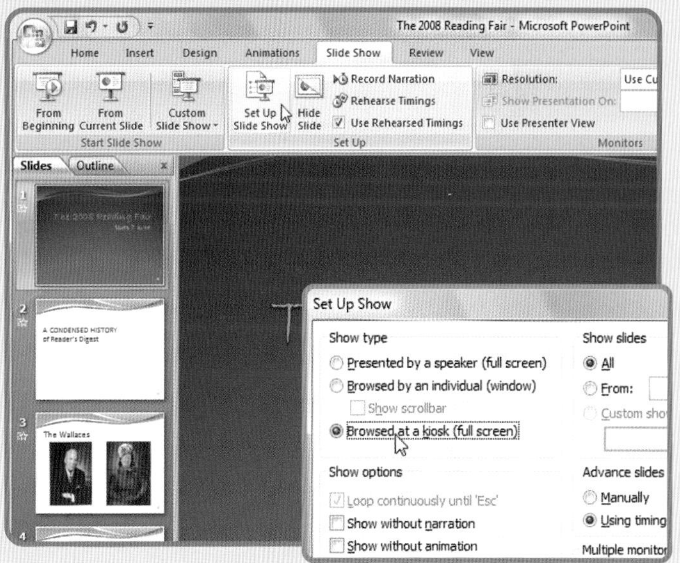

# Hyperlinks & buttons

The slides in a slide show don't necessarily have to appear consecutively from beginning to end. You can incorporate interactive elements which allow viewers to jump back and forth between slides, display additional information or even link to a particular Web site – all at the click of a mouse. Hyperlinks and buttons are the features that make this possible.

**SEE ALSO ...**

- *Slide shows* p92

## WORKING WITH LINKS

**Open a finished presentation containing multiple slides. Your computer must be connected to the Internet in order to add a Web site link to your presentation.**

### Inserting hyperlinks

A **hyperlink** allows you to click on some text or an object on your slide and automatically open a file, Web page or another slide. You can also use a hyperlink to start a new email message. In your presentation, hyperlinked text appears underlined.

To insert a hyperlink, select a word on a slide and click on the **Insert** tab and then on **Hyperlink** in the Links group. The Insert Hyperlink dialogue box lets you specify what the hyperlink will link to.

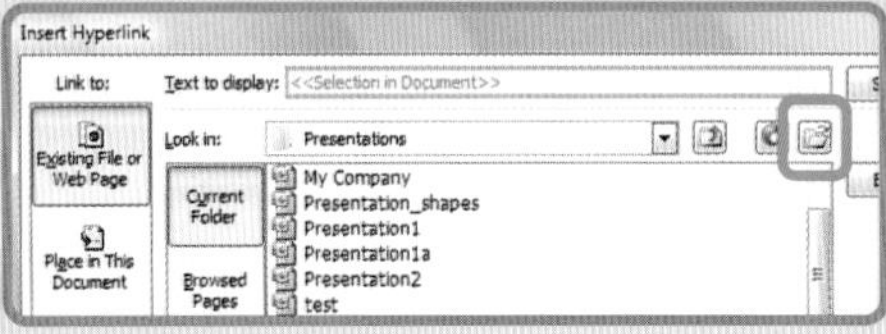


If it is going to link to another PowerPoint presentation, you can link it directly to a specific slide within that presentation. Simply navigate to the other PowerPoint file, select it and click on the **Bookmark** icon. Then choose the slide that you want to link to in the Select Place in Document dialogue box.

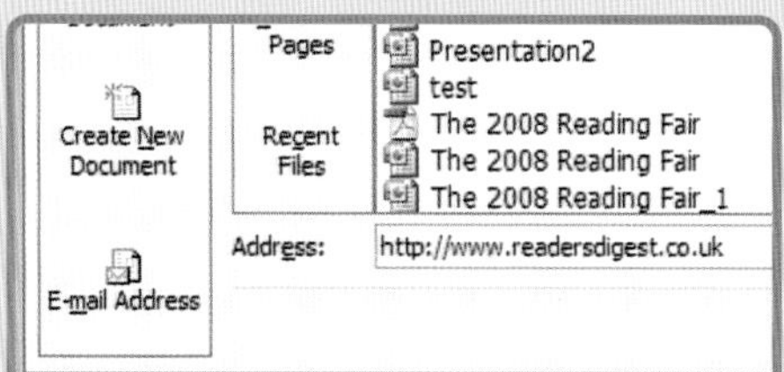


To link to a Web site, enter its address in the 'Address' box of the Insert Hyperlink dialogue box. When a user clicks on the link, they will be taken directly to the site.

### Links to other slides of the current presentation

To link to other slides in your presentation, click on the **Insert** tab and click on **Hyperlink** in the Links group. Click on **Place in This Document** under 'Link to' in the left-hand column and then select the slide that will be shown when the link is clicked on.

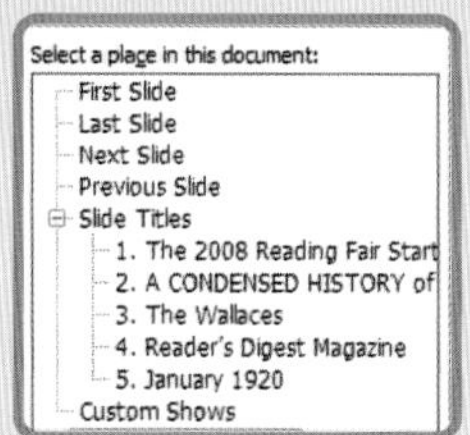


### Creating a new document

Instead of linking to an existing document, you can create a new document that will be opened when the link is clicked on. This new document could contain extra information concerning a specific point, for example. Click on **Create New Document** in the 'Link to' column of the Insert Hyperlink dialogue box and enter a file name in the 'Name of new document' box. Make sure you use a common file extension, for example .doc for a Word document and .ppt or .pptx for a PowerPoint presentation. Click on **Change** to select a different location for the new document to be saved in. The 'When to edit' option lets you choose whether to add content to the new document immediately, or at a later stage. Click on **OK** to confirm your choices.

If you select **Edit the new document now**, the relevant program will start up automatically.

### Email addresses

You can also insert a hyperlink which will allow viewers to send an email. This is useful if your presentation is advertising a club, for example, because prospective members can then contact you from within the presentation itself. To add this hyperlnk, click **E-mail Address** in the 'Link to' column of the Insert Hyperlink dialogue box. Enter the recipient's email address in the 'E-mail address' box. When the link is clicked upon, the computer's email program opens automatically. You can even fill in the subject line of the email in advance.

## Working with buttons

As well as turning words and objects into hyperlinks, you can add links in the form of buttons to your slides. Clicking on a button is the same as clicking on a hyperlink, taking the viewer to another presentation slide or opening a document or Web page. Buttons can also be used to end a slide show.

## Adding buttons

To add a button, click on the **Insert** tab, then on **Shapes** in the Illustrations group. From the

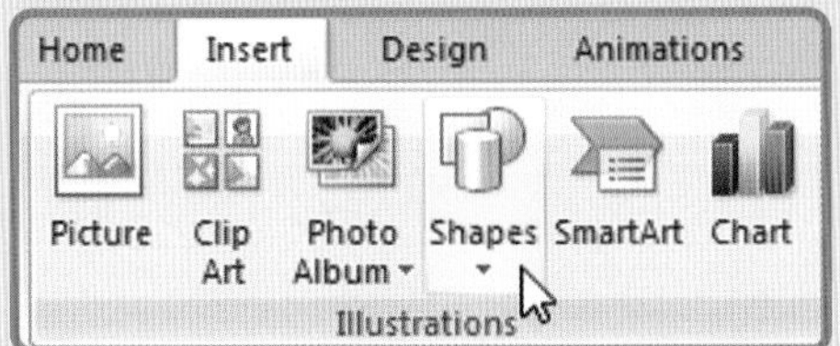


drop-down menu choose from a selection of different icons under 'Action Buttons'.

There are a number of pre-defined action buttons to choose from, including 'Forward',

'Back', 'Home' (selected here), 'Movie' and 'Sound'. There is also a customisable button. Choose an icon that suits the the hyperlink it will activate. The cursor turns into a cross. Move the cursor to the place you want to insert the button and click. The Action Settings dialogue box appears. You can select the Mouse Click or Mouse Over tab. If you choose Mouse Click, the button is activated when clicked upon. If you select Mouse Over the viewer need only move the cursor over the button in order to activate it.

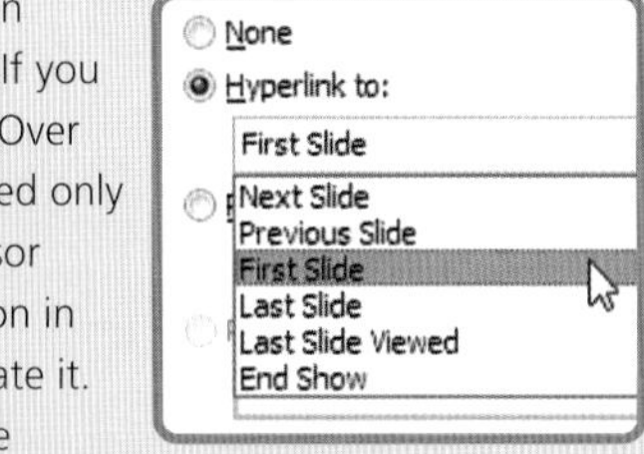


Click on the **Mouse Click** tab and select the 'Hyperlink to' option. Use the drop-down menu to specify what should happen when the button is clicked. It could, for example, take you back to the first slide or to a Web site.

If you select the 'Run program' option instead of 'Hyperlink to', you can enter the path to a program that will be launched when the button is clicked on. You might want to launch your email program, for example, so that viewers can send an

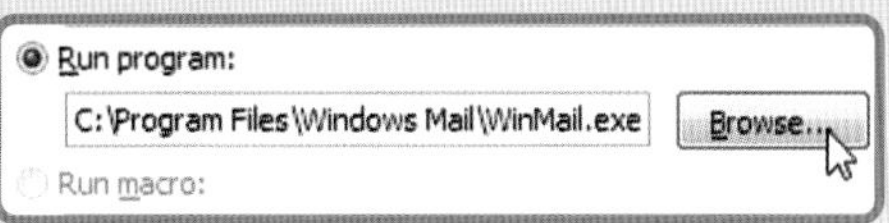


email. If you are not sure where the program is located, click on the **Browse** button to find it.

## Combining buttons with sound effects

If you want to play a sound effect when the button is clicked upon, tick the 'Play sound' checkbox in the Action Settings dialogue box. Choose the sound that you want to use from the drop-down menu and, when you are happy with the settings you have chosen, click on **OK** to confirm them.

## Customising buttons

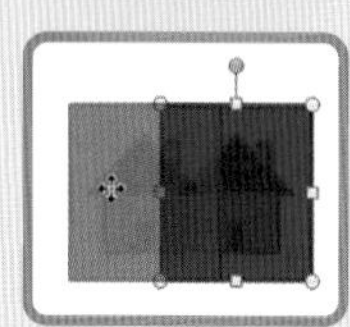

When the button is displayed on the slide you can change its size and scale by clicking and dragging the white sizing handles. The green dot above the button allows you to rotate the position of the button on the slide.

To put the button in a new position, move the mouse over the button so that the cursor changes into a four-headed arrow. Click and drag it to its new location, and release the mouse.

To change the appearance of the button – its colour, for example – right-click on it, and choose **Format Shape** from the drop-down menu. In the Format Shape dialogue box that appears, select 'Fill' in the left pane, click on the 'Color' drop-down menu and select a new colour from the palette. You can make other changes in the Format Shape dialogue box if you wish. Click on **Close** to finish.

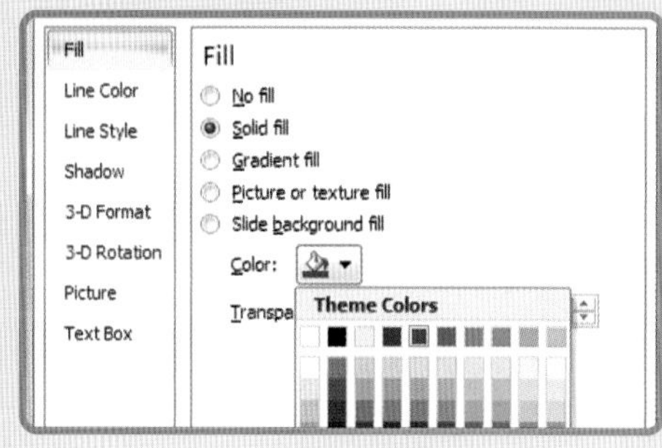

### Key word

***A hyperlink is a link used to connect to another document or object, such as a Web site or a slide in a different presentation. It's the digital equivalent of a cross-reference or footnote in a book or printed article.***

### Deleting hyperlinks and buttons

To remove a hyperlink associated with some text, right-click on the underlined word and select 'Remove Hyperlink' in the context menu. To delete a button, click on it to select it and then press the **Delete** key on the keyboard.

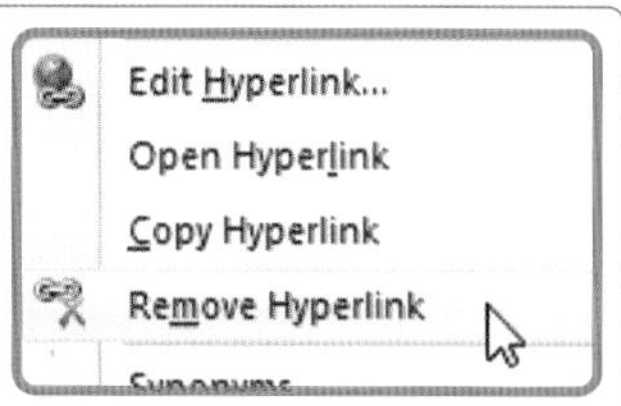

# Saving as a PDF

A PDF (Portable Document Format) file is a popular way of sending documents electronically, because it is a small size file and a recipient can open a PDF even if they don't have the software used to create it. PowerPoint 2007 has an 'add-in' that lets you save documents into PDF format but you need Adobe Acrobat Reader to view a PDF (this can be downloaded for free).

**SEE ALSO ...**

- *Saving your work p24*

**BEFORE YOU START**

*Start up PowerPoint using an icon shortcut on the Desktop or by clicking on the **Start** button and selecting it from the menu. When PowerPoint has opened, click on the **Office** button.*

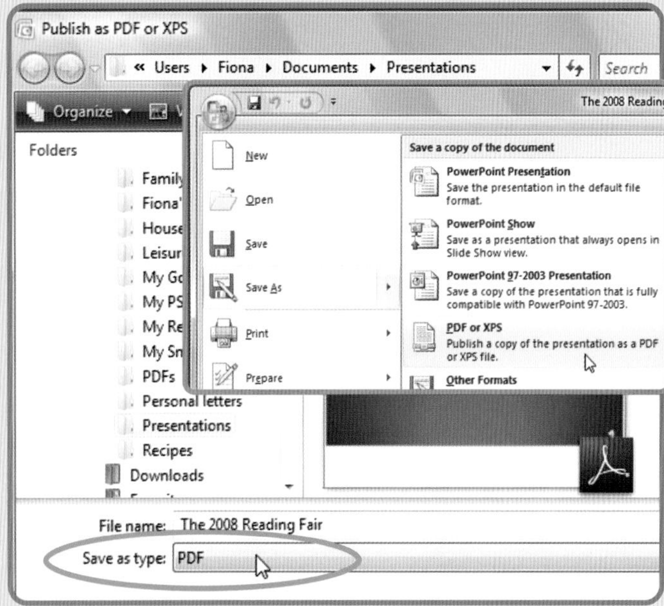


**1** Open a Microsoft Office 2007 PowerPoint presentation and click on the **Office** button, then on **Save As** in the left pane. Select **PDF or XPS** from the options in the right pane. In the Publish as PDF or XPS dialogue box, name your file and make sure the 'PDF' option is selected in the 'Save as type' panel.

**2** Below the 'Save as type' panel of the dialogue box, you can add a tick next to 'Open file after publishing' to automatically view the PDF once it has been created. Next to this option, set the optimisation level that you want. The default option 'Standard (publishing online and printing)' is suitable for most purposes. Now click on **Options** to adjust or set any additional options before creating the PDF.

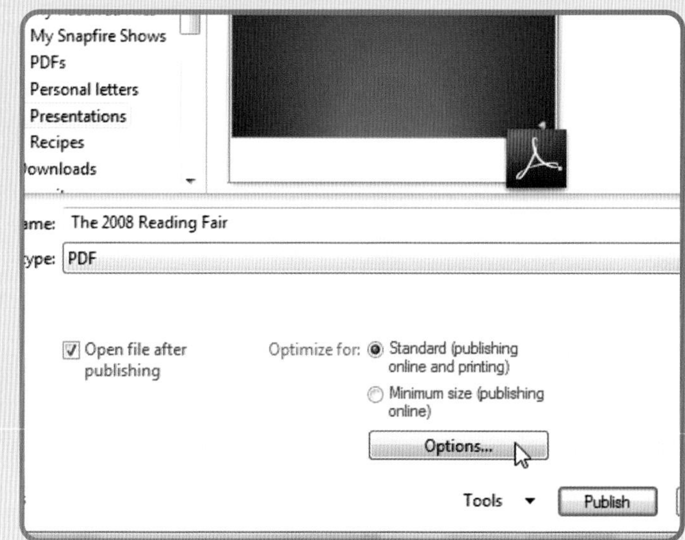

### Bright idea

***To save or export a file to PDF you need to have the appropriate 'add-in' installed on your computer. Click on the*** *Office* ***button, then on*** *Save As.* ***If you see the option 'PDF or XPS' in the right-hand pane then the add-in has been installed. If you can't see it in this pane, click on*** *Find add-ins for other file formats* ***to download it for free from the Microsoft Office Web site.***

### Expert advice

In order to view a PDF, you need to have Adobe Acrobat Reader installed on your PC. You can download it for free from **www.adobe.com**. Remember, any animations, transitions, sound and video will be missing in the PDF version of the presentation.

**3** In most cases, the default option settings will be adequate. Under 'Range', you can choose whether to publish all slides, the current slide or a selection of slides. The options under 'Publish what' allow you to set the format as 'Slides', 'Handouts', 'Notes pages' or 'Outline view'. Make your changes and click on **OK**. Click on **Publish** to complete the process.

**4** A progress bar displays while the PDF is created. If you put a tick next to 'Open file after publishing' in the Publish as PDF or XPS dialogue box (see Step 2) your newly created PDF file will be automatically opened in Adobe Acrobat Reader. You are now able to send this presentation to someone, as an email attachment, for example, knowing that they will be able to open, view and print it out.

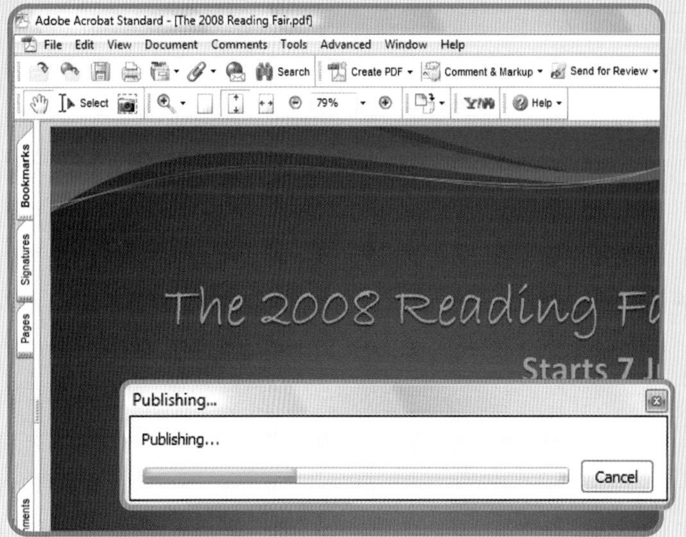

**Active window** The window in which you are working. Clicking on an inactive window brings it to the front of the screen and activates it. *See Window*.
**Adjustment handle** The white square or round handles that appear at the corners and sides of text boxes, shapes and placeholders when you have them selected. You can adjust the dimensions of an object by clicking on the adjustment handles and dragging them to a new position. *See Sizing handle*.
**Alignment** The position of text in a text box, shape or placeholder. Text can be aligned to the centre, left or right or it can be justified.
**Alt key** The key found to the left of the Spacebar on the keyboard, which activates a command when pressed in combination with certain other keys.
**Animation** By adding animations to an object or text you can make it appear, disappear and move around the screen when you set up your presentation to run as a slide show. *See Slide transition*.
**Arrow keys** The four directional keys at the bottom right of the keyboard which move the cursor around the screen.
**AutoCorrect** This feature finds and corrects common spelling and grammar errors as you type.
**AutoFormat** A feature used to apply formatting according to the settings that you have previously created and saved.

# B

**Background** A colour or effect positioned on a slide as a layer on top of which all other elements are placed.
**Backspace key** This key deletes text to the left of the cursor insertion point. *See Delete key*.
**Bitmap** A term used to describe photographs and graphics which are made up of tiny individual dots or pixels. Common bitmap file formats include BMP and TIFF. *See Vector graphic*.
**Bullet point** A small graphic, often a black dot, used to indicate separate points within a list.
**Button** A symbol on the screen that, when clicked on, performs a function such as opening a dialogue box.

# C

**Caps Lock** Press this key once to make the letters you type appear as capitals. Press the key again to return to standard characters. *See Shift key*.
**Cell** The basic element of a table, generally a small, rectangular area, into which text or figures are entered.
**Chart** A graphical representation of data, such as a graph, that can be placed on a PowerPoint slide.
**Clip Art** Pictures, photographs and drawings that are supplied with Microsoft Office programs. These can be inserted into presentations and then resized and manipulated.
**Clipboard** Text and any other objects that you have cut or copied are stored on the Clipboard. You can store 24 different items on the Clipboard at any one time.
**Close** A command to shut down the file that is active, but not the whole program.
**Content layou**t A slide layout containing placeholders for pictures, Clip Art, tables, charts and other objects.
**Context menu** A menu that is displayed when you right-click on an object. The commands on the menu vary according to the type of object you have clicked on.
**Contextual tabs** These are tabs that appear only when a specific action has been carried out. If, for example, you click on a text box to select it, the Drawing Tools contextual tab will then be displayed above the Ribbon.
**Copy** A command used to temporarily copy text or an object onto the Clipboard. The keyboard shortcut to copy is Ctrl + C.
**Crop** A function used to trim the edges of a picture in order to make it smaller. Click on a picture on a slide and then click on the Crop button in the Size group to activate the function.
**Cursor** A marker – usually a flashing vertical line – which appears whenever you are inserting or editing text on a slide. Also called the 'Insertion point'.
**Custom slide shows** This feature allows you to create multiple versions of the same presentation. Each version can contain a selection of the slides found in the original file. The different versions are saved with the original presentation.
**Cut** To remove selected text or objects from a presentation to the Clipboard, from where you can paste them in another location. The keyboard shortcut to cut is Ctrl + X.

**Delete** To remove a file or folder from your computer, or a picture or section of text from your presentation. If you accidentally delete an object while working in PowerPoint, you can restore it by clicking on the Undo button in the Quick Access Toolbar. The keyboard shortcut to delete is Ctrl + Z.
**Delete key** A key used to delete text to the right of the cursor insertion point.
**Design Tab** A tab on the Ribbon which holds options for themes, page set-up and background.
**Desktop** The main working area of a computer screen which is displayed whenever you open Windows. Programs, folders and documents on the Desktop are represented by icons.
**Dialogue box** A window that appears on screen containing a message generated by the program you are currently using. Dialogue boxes often prompt users to adjust settings or enter certain information.

**Dialogue box launcher** A small diagonal arrow found to the bottom right of a group on the Ribbon. Click on the arrow to display a dialogue box containing all of the commands related to the group.
**Documents** A folder accessed via the Windows Start menu and in which documents that you require frequently are saved.
**Double-click** To press and release the left mouse button twice in quick succession. This is most often used to open files and folders, and to activate programs.
**Drag** A mouse action used to highlight text, reshape objects, or move an object or file. Click and, with the mouse button held down, move the mouse as required. Release the mouse button to finish the action. When moving an object or file, this is known as 'drag and drop'.
**Drawing Tools** A contextual ribbon of commands, accessed when an image is clicked on, providing options for manipulating the image.
**Duplicate Slide** An exact copy of a slide, which is created by right-clicking on a slide in Slides view and selecting 'Duplicate' from the context menu. The copy of the slide is then inserted directly after the original.

## E

**Edit** To make a change to an element in a presentation. Also to alter the settings for a program.
**Effect** *See Animation*.
**End key** Pressing this key takes you to the last slide of the presentation.

## F

**File** Any program, text document, presentation, image or other item that is stored on a computer's hard disk.
**File format** The way in which files created by different programs are saved. *See POT, PPT and PPTX*.
**Find** A command used to locate particular words and phrases used in a presentation.
**Folder** An electronic storage location on the PC's hard disk, designed to help you keep related files together.
**Font** A specific style and set of characters that are characteristic of a typeface such as Times New Roman or Helvetica.
**Footer** The area found at the bottom of every slide which can contain information such as the slide number, the date or the time. *See Header*.
**Format** To alter the appearance of text by changing the font, the font size and the line spacing between text.
**Function keys** The 12 keys found in the top row of the keyboard, from F1 to F12. Their functions depend on the particular program that you are using at that time. For example, in many programs pressing F1 opens up the help screen.

## G

**Graphic** The collective term for any type of digital image, including pictures, photographs, illustrations and Clip Art.
**Gridlines** A series of invisible horizontal and vertical lines, along which objects on a slide are automatically aligned. You can show this grid by clicking on the View tab and selecting 'Gridlines' in the Show/Hide group. For a more precise grid, right-click on a blank area of a slide and select 'Grid and Guides' from the drop-down menu. The dialogue box that appears allows you to adjust the spacing of the gridlines but it must be within a range of 0.125cm to 5cm.
**Group** The categories into which buttons for PowerPoint tasks have been organised on the Ribbon. *See Ribbon*.
**Grouping** The act of combining several objects into one item that can then be enlarged, reduced or otherwise manipulated as a single unit.

## H

**Handout** Print-outs of your presentation which you can distribute to your audience. A single page of a handout contains up to six miniaturised slides.
**Header** The area at the top of a handout or notes page into which you can enter text. *See Footer*.
**Help key** Usually the F1 key on the keyboard, this accesses advice and information on tasks. *See Function keys*.
**Hide Slide** A command found in the Set Up group under the Slide Show tab, which is used to hide individual slides within a slide show. The hidden slides are not deleted from the PowerPoint document permanently, and they can be restored to the slide show by selecting the command again.
**Highlight** To select an item such as text or an image by clicking and dragging the cursor over the item. *See Drag*.
**Home key** Press this key to go to the first slide in the presentation.
**Home tab** The first tab on the Ribbon. Here you can access the Cut, Copy and Paste buttons, select Fonts and Font sizes, and change the alignment of text.
**Hyperlink** A piece of underlined text or an object which when clicked on will take you to a Web site or into another presentation or a document.

## I

**Indent** An indent is used to move either the first or all lines of a paragraph in from the left margin. When all lines of a paragraph except the first line are indented it is known as a hanging indent.
**Indentation mark** *See Tab stop*.
**Inkjet printer** A type of printer that works by squirting tiny drops of black and/or coloured ink onto the surface of the paper. Most home printers use inkjets.
**Insertion point** *See Cursor*.

**Italic** A font style whereby the letters are slightly tilted to the right. Italics are often used to emphasise words and sentences.

## K

**Keyboard shortcut** A combination of keys pressed simultaneously to activate a specific command (Ctrl + S for 'Save', for example).

## L

**Laser printer** A type of printer that uses a laser to etch images onto a drum and then transfers the images onto paper. It gives a higher-quality printout than that from an inkjet printer.

**Live Preview** A feature that lets you see how a formatting change, such as a new colour or font, will look before you commit to it.

## M

**Master** A Master is used to control how the slides in a presentation are viewed on screen. There are four types of Master: the Slide Master, Title Master, Handout Master and Notes Master.

**Maximise** To increase the size of a window so that it fills the entire screen area. To return a maximised window back to its original size click on the Restore Down button.

**Minimise** To reduce a window to a button on the Taskbar. Click on the minimised window to restore it to its original size.

**Mouse pointer** A small arrow that moves around the screen as you move the mouse. The arrow changes into other symbols – such as a hand, pen or cross – depending on the program you are working in or the task you are performing.

## N

**Narration** A spoken soundtrack that can be recorded and used to accompany a slide show presentation. It is very useful in self-running presentations and helpful for absentees who missed an original presentation.

**Normal view** The default view for looking at slides. Normal view displays the active slide, an outline of all the slides on the left-hand side of the screen and the Notes pane under the active slide.

**Notes** Every slide in a presentation, has a notes page displayed at the bottom of the window in Normal view. It is where the presentation giver enters information that can be referred to when giving the presentation. Notes pages can be printed separately and are not visible to the audience during a slide show.

**Numbered list** Similar to a list using bullet points, text is structured in an indented list of consecutively numbered points, from 1 onwards.

## O

**Object** Elements on a slide – text boxes, pictures or charts – are known as objects. You can position objects anywhere on the slide, and change their size, fill colours and outlines for example.

**Office button** A round button found at the top left of Office 2007 programs that gives access to certain basic functions, including open, print and save, as well as some extra features such as on-line templates.

**Open** The command used to access files and folders.

**Organisation Chart** A special type of chart used to represent hierarchical structures, such as a family tree, graphically.

**Orientation** An option used when printing documents to print the page out in a landscape or portrait format.

## P

**Package for CD** A feature that allows you to burn a presentation directly on to a CD. You can then put the CD into any PC to display your presentation, even one that doesn't have PowerPoint installed.

**Page Up/Page Down** Keys used to move the cursor up or down several lines of text at a time.

**Paste** To insert text or objects that have been cut or copied to the Office Clipboard into a new location on a slide or onto a different slide. The keyboard shortcut is Ctrl + V.

**Pen tools** Electronic tools which the speaker can use to write on their slides while presenting a slide show. They are useful for highlighting a point or adding a note. The tools are accessed by moving the mouse.

**Placeholder** All elements on a slide including the title, text and images are placed within placeholders. These are indicated by their dotted frames, and can be positioned and altered in the same way as objects.

**Point size** A standard scale for measuring font size. A font may be described as 12pt, for example.

**POT** Standard file format used to save PowerPoint templates.

**PPT** File format previously used to save all PowerPoint presentations.

**PPTX** Standard file format used to save PowerPoint Office 2007 presentations.

**Presentation** Term used to describe a PowerPoint document. A presentation comprises one or more slides, and can be presented on screen, projected on to a projector screen or printed out. *See Handout*.

**Print Preview** A feature within the Print dialogue box that shows how the slides will look when they are printed out.

**Quick Access Toolbar** A customisable toolbar found at the top left of a PowerPoint window. By default it contains the

Save, Undo and Repeat/Redo commands but you can add extra buttons for commands that you commonly use.

# R

**Radio button** A small round circle next to an option that needs to be clicked on to select the option. If there is more than one radio button associated with a given feature, you can only select one option at any one time.
**Recycle Bin** A special folder on the Desktop used to store deleted files and folders. The contents of the Recycle Bin are only permanently removed when the bin is emptied.
**Reduce** To make an open window smaller so that it no longer fills the entire screen.
**Rehearse Timings** Feature used to practise giving a presentation and set the length of time that each slide is displayed for in a slide show.
**Replace Font** A feature used to replace every instance of a specific font in a presentation with another font. This command is accessed in the Editing group found under the Home tab.
**Return key** The large key on the right-hand side of the main block of keys on the keyboard, used to produce paragraph breaks. It can also be used to execute commands instead of clicking on an 'OK' button.
**Review Tab** A tab on the ribbon which contains commands for proofing the content of a presentation, for example 'Spelling' and 'Thesaurus'.
**Ribbon** A new toolbar-focused way of working in Office 2007. Click on the tabs at the top of the Ribbon to access buttons for tasks organised into groups by their similar function.
**Right-click** To press and release the right mouse button. In PowerPoint, this displays a menu of options. The options differ depending on the item on which you clicked.
**Rotating handle** A small green dot that is found on the edge of an object when it is selected. When clicked on it is used to rotate an object on a slide.

# S

**Save** A command used to copy a presentation from the computer's memory to the hard disk or other drive in order to keep it filed and possibly use it again later.
**Save as** A command to save an existing document under another file name, in another file format or in a new place.
**Scroll bar** Bars along the right and bottom edges of the window which allow you to navigate around a document or presentation. Click on the arrows at each end of a scroll bar or drag the block to move more quickly around the window.
**Select** To click on objects and pictures in order to move or adjust them. You can also select text, pictures or table cells by dragging the cursor over them. *See Drag*.
**Shapes** A selection of ready-made graphic shapes that you can insert into a presentation, and which can contain text.
**Shift key** This key serves various functions. When held down, it allows you to type capital letters and access the symbols on the number keys. Pressed in combination with other keys, the Shift key also provides quick access to some features (for example, pressing Shift + Alt + T inserts the current time in the active document or slide).
**Sizing handle** Small squares that appear at the corners and edges of objects such as graphics when they are selected. Use the sizing handles to adjust an object's size.
**Slide** PowerPoint presentations are comprised of one or more slides, which are equivalent to the pages of a Word document. Text, graphics and all other elements are positioned on the slides.
**Slide layout** The slide layout determines how different elements are arranged on a slide. Slide layouts contain text placeholders (such as the title of the slide and bulleted lists) or other types of content (such as pictures and tables).
**Slide master** *See Master*.
**Slide show** A way of presenting your slides to an audience either on a computer monitor or via a projector.
**Slide Sorter view** In this view, the slides of a presentation are shown as thumbnail images. Slide Sorter view is particularly useful if you want to re-order slides, set slide transitions or hide slides.
**Slide title** The placeholder for the title of a slide. In Normal view, the slide title is also shown in the Outline tab.
**Slide transition** Effects that can be added to a slide show to animate the transition from one slide to the next.
**Spacebar** The wide key at the bottom of the keyboard used to insert spaces between words, letters and numbers.

# T

**3D Effects** A feature used to apply three-dimensional effects to objects on a slide such as text boxes and shapes.
**Table** Groups of cells arranged in rows and columns and containing text or images. Putting information into a table can help to make it more accessible.
**Tab** (1) Short for 'tabulate'. A feature for positioning text at various set distances from the left-hand margin.
**Tab** (2) A heading found on the Ribbon (also known as a Commmand Tab). Clicking on a tab gives access to groups of buttons for related commands. *See Ribbon*.
**Tab key** The key to the left of the 'Q' key, used to position text at preset intervals within a text box, to grade entries in a list or to move between cells in a table.

**Tab stop** The marker on the ruler indicating the alignment of text in a document, for example in a list.
**Taskbar** The strip, usually positioned along the bottom of the Windows Desktop, which contains the Start button as well as buttons for all open programs and documents.
**Task pane** A panel that appears on the right-hand side of the screen providing access to commonly used commands. There are different task panes for different tasks, for example inserting Clip Art or using the Thesaurus. The task pane appears when you select a related command on the Ribbon.
**Template** The slides of a presentation which can be used as the basis for the presentation that you are creating. PowerPoint has a selection of preset templates available or you can produce templates from your own presentations. *See POT*.
**Text box** An object in which you can place text or images. *See Shapes*.
**Theme Colours** Each theme comes complete with four text and background colours, six accent colours and two hyperlink colours. You can create a new collection of colours and save it for use in any future presentations. *See Themes*.
**Themes** These are preset design styles that you can apply to the slides in your presentation. Each theme includes fonts, colours and special effects for all of the elements that are found within a presentation, including the slide background, text, lines, drop shadows, titles, fills, highlighted items and hyperlinks.
**Thesaurus** An alphabetical list of words and their synonyms and antonyms, structured in much the same way as a dictionary.
**Timing** In a self-running slide show, the timing setting determines how long each slide is displayed. Each slide can be set to appear for a particular length of time, independent of the others.
**Toolbar** A floating window with buttons that access commands and features. The Mini Toolbar, with formatting options, appears when you move the mouse pointer over highlighted text.

**Undo** A feature that allows you to undo one or more of the last actions you have carried out.
**USB Memory stick** A small portable memory storage device that can be connected to a USB port of a PC. It can be used to transfer files from one computer to another.

**Vector graphic** Pictures comprised of solid lines, curves and flat shapes are called vector graphics. Unlike bitmaps, vector graphics can be enlarged to any size without compromising the image quality.
**View** Click on the View tab to access options that allow you to alter the way a presentation is displayed on screen.

## W

**Window** The self-contained viewing and work area of an open program or presentation.
**Windows Explorer** A program for viewing the contents of a computer in a single window.
**WordArt** A feature that allows you to add colourful, decorative detail to text in your presentation.

## Z

**Zoom** A command used to enlarge or reduce the view of the slide displayed on screen.

# Index

**How to do just about anything in Microsoft® PowerPoint – Office 2007**

**was edited and designed by The Reader's Digest Association Limited, London**



We are committed both to the quality of our products and the service we provide to our customers. We value your comments, so please do contact us on **08705 113366**, or via our Web site at **www.readersdigest.co.uk**
If you have any comments or suggestions about this book, e-mail us at
**gbeditorial@readersdigest.co.uk**



Origination: Mullis Morgan Imaging Ltd, London

Printed and bound in China

**Book code 400-380 UP0000-1**
**ISBN 978 0 276 44383 1**
**Oracle code 250012384H.00.24**